VOLUME SIX
SOLDAT

The World War II
German Combat Collector's Handbook

Equipping the
WAFFEN-*ϟϟ* PANZER DIVISIONS 1942 - 1945

by

Richard W. Mundt
and
Cyrus A. Lee

Pictorial Histories Publishing Co., Inc.
Missoula, Montana

COPYRIGHT ©1997 CYRUS A. LEE and RICHARD W. MUNDT
All rights reserved. No part of this book may be used or reproduced without the written permission of the publisher.

LIBRARY OF CONGRESS
CATALOG CARD NO. 88-90959
ISBN 1-57510-018-5

Printed in the U.S.A.
First Printing: January 1997

Photography by:
Cyrus Lee, Frank Thayer, John Newman, Ralph Heinz
Edited by Steve Rusiecki
Typography, Layout and Waffen-// Runes by: Marshall Wise
Artwork by: Tim Parker

Companion Volumes:
Vol. I - Equipping the German Army Foot Soldier in Europe in 1939 - 1942
Vol. II - Equipping the German Army Foot Soldier in Europe in 1943
Vol. III - Equipping the German Army Foot Soldier in Europe in 1944 -1945
Vol. V - Uniforms and Insignia of Panzerkorps Großdeutschland 1939 -1945
Volume XI. - The Reproductions - The Post War Years

Companion Series:
CANUCK—The World War II Canadian Military Collector's Handbooks

Future Companion Volumes:
Vol. IV - Equipping the German Army Foot Soldier in Southern Europe and North Africa 1940 -1945
Vol. VII - Equipping the Waffen-// Panzergrenadier Regiments 1942 - 1945
Vol. VIII - Equipping the German Airborne Soldier 1935 - 1945
Vol. X - Corrections and Additions

Future Companion Series:
G.I.—The World War II American Military Collector's Handbooks
TOMMY—The World War II British Collector's Handbooks
IVAN—The World War II Soviet Collector's Handbooks
MUSKITIER— The World War I German Army Collector's Handbooks
POILU—The World War I French Military Collector's Handbooks
DOUGHBOY—The World War I American Military Collector's Handbooks

Pictorial Histories Publishing Co., Inc.
713 South Third St. West, Missoula, MT 59801

Preface

It was in Frankfurt, Germany during the late 80s when I talked to Richard Mundt about a Waffen-♯♯ book. By 1992 he had completed his research and draft on his book about the Waffen-♯♯ Panzer Regiments. Time passed as the SOLDAT series began to take root, and new books began to appear on a somewhat regular schedule. During the early months of 1995 I began to assemble Richard's work. Striving to touch new areas, this SOLDAT volume focuses on the Panzer soldiers of the seven Waffen-♯♯ Armored Divisions. Some of the original photos capture pre- and early war periods and are included as part of the historical development of the units and individuals towards the time of the formation of the armored divisions.

I am pleased with the direction that SOLDAT is taking as more and more hobbyists join in to help produce information for other hobbyists. I want SOLDAT to retain the things that first attracted readers to the series and to give more detail and to make more historical connections with the German soldier of World War II

As with all SOLDAT books, I ask for your comments and constructive criticism. The impact of the ideas from hobbyists has continued to drive the series; no comment is left unpondered and many are acted upon.

Cyrus A. Lee

Introduction

The intent of this book is to describe and illustrate the uniforms, insignia, and equipment of the Panzer regiments of the seven Waffen-*ϟϟ* Armored Divisions. A number of private, and unpublished, photos have been included to aid in this illustration. This increased use of period photos is attributable to the rarity of the subject matter, difficulty in accessing private collections, and the authors' desires to increase the historical flavor of the book. This work concerns itself with the soldiers of the Panzer Divisions from 1942 until 1945, but aside from small pieces of insignia the uniforms of all Waffen-*ϟϟ* soldiers were the same.

Not all areas of uniforms and field gear have been covered; only those that could be found with *ϟϟ* markings or that were new and of interest are included. Other items are mentioned and may be studied in other SOLDAT books. Only weapons that have not been covered in previous works have been included. As with other SOLDAT books, many items have been photographed on live models to give the reader a view of how they would look in action.

This book makes no attempt, like many others, to homogenize history by stating "must" statements concerning how things were. Uniforms and equipment of the Third Reich were manufactured by a number of different contractors who were often faced with impoverished supplies. The study and handling of original items shows that there were variances in the materials and construction of uniforms, insignia, and equipment.

SOLDAT has been created from the research of historical and contemporary writing, interviews with veterans of the Waffen-*ϟϟ*, research compiled and submitted by contemporary historians and collectors, and photographs of items in private and public collections.

Acknowledgments

This work would not have been possible without the time, effort and interest of a number of veterans and collectors. I wish to express my special thanks to the former soldiers of the Waffen-// who allowed me to visit in their homes or at reunions. I thank them for trusting me with their rare and interesting personal photographs. Special thanks go to architect Karl-Heinz Hellman whose artistic talents created the camouflage rank table.

I thank a number of German and Danish collectors who wish to remain anonymous for fear of possible repercussions in their homelands. I thank Frank Thayer for photographing the rare „Totenkopf" Divisional insignia.

I also want to give thanks to Marika Toth, a very special lady who gave me the confidence to follow through on my research and complete the work. Listed below in alphabetical order, I thank the following individuals:

- Christina Biendl geb. Schneider
- Malcom Bowers
- Peter Jenkins
- Jens Link
- Christoph Schulz
- Rick Squeri
- Frank Thayer

The following former soldiers of the Waffen-//:

- Strm. Rudi Behme
- Uscha. Franz Gajdosch
- Ustuf. Joachim Glade
- Strm. Martin Glade
- Uscha. Josef Hannappel
- Hscha. Fritz "Bello" Haupt
- Uscha. Karl - Heinz Hellmann
- Hstuf. Herbert Höfler
- Ostuf. Horst Schneider

- ❖ Stubf. Hans Siegel
- ❖ The Dezember '44 Museum
- ❖ The Veterans of the 1. SS Panzerkorp
- ❖ Martin Glade
- ❖ George Gross

Richard Mundt

Contents

Preface iii
Introduction iv
Acknowledgments v
Foreward/Vorwort x
The Waffen-ϟϟ Panzer Service Jacket 8
The Waffen-ϟϟ Panzer Service Trouser 14
The Waffen-ϟϟ Field Gray Panzer Service Uniform 16
The Waffen-ϟϟ Issue Shirt and Necktie 27
The Waffen-ϟϟ Belt Buckles 29
The Waffen-ϟϟ Leather Belts 33
The Waffen-ϟϟ Herringbone Twill (HBT) Panzer Service Uniform 35
The Waffen-ϟϟ Reversible Camouflage Panzer Overall 38
The Waffen-ϟϟ Reversible Winter Panzer Overall 40
The Italian Camouflage and Naval Foul Weather Uniforms 41
Waffen-ϟϟ Rank and their equivalents 45
Waffen-ϟϟ Field Cap, Old Pattern 48
The Waffen-ϟϟ Field Cap, New Pattern 49
The Waffen-ϟϟ Peaked Uniform Cap 53
The Waffen-ϟϟ Peaked Field Cap for NCOs 54
The Waffen-ϟϟ Metal Insignia for Peaked Caps 58
The Waffen-ϟϟ Camouflage Field Cap 59
The Waffen-ϟϟ Model 1943 Field Cap and its Insignia 60
ϟϟ Panzer Regiment 1 64
ϟϟ-Panzer Regiment 2 69
ϟϟ-Panzer Regiment 3 87

SS-Panzer Regiment 5 94
SS-Panzer Regiment 9, 9. SS-Panzer Division „Hohenstaufen" and
    SS-Panzer Regiment 10/ 10. SS-Panzer Division „Frundsberg" 96
SS-Panzer Abteilung 11 „Hermann von Salza"/
    11. SS-Freiwilligen Panzergrenadier Division „Nordland" 99
SS-Panzer Regiment 12/ 12. SS-Panzer Division „Hitlerjugend" 101
The Waffen-SS Cuff Title 106
Construction of Waffen-SS Shoulder Board Insignia 110
The Waffen-SS Collar Rank Insignia 112
The Waffen-SS Collar Runic Insignia 114
The Waffen-SS Sleeve Eagle 117
The Waffen-SS Sleeve Rank 121
The Waffen-SS Rank Insignia for Camouflage Uniforms 122
The Waffen-SS Honor Chevron 123

Der alte Hase

Panzer Regiments 3
Understanding Waffen-SS Ranks and Rank Insignia 4
Officers Belt and Buckle 31
Marking Headgear 49
Unit Insignia 66
On Point With a King Tiger 124
SS-Panzers in Normandy; An SS-Panzer Platoon Leader in
    the Roncey Pocket, July 1944. 131

Lernen durch Erfahrung

Soutache Braid 49
Colored Piping 53
Slip-on Shoulder Titles 65
„Hitlerjugend" Cuff titles 101
Artificial Silk 105

SS-Hauptsturmführer Michael Wittmann
22 · 4 · 14 - 8 · 8 · 44
270 Tank, Assault Gun and Anti-Tank Gun Victor

Foreward/Vorwort

*T*he author has laboriously concentrated on the subject very thoroughly. He uncovers details that even the former men who wore the different uniforms cannot remember exactly. In action these things were of no importance. Whichever uniforms proved practical or were available were worn.

In this work, not only is every detail of form, cut, and appearance described but also the different types of manufacture and raw material used in production. The different types of uniforms are specifically classified for officers, non-commissioned officers, and enlisted men.

Not only the tankers who once proudly wore these uniforms can thank the author for this historical documentation in words and illustrations. It is a reference work on a specific subject, a work for all who have an interest in military science.

---

*D*er Verfasser hat sich in mühevoller Arbeit gründlich und ausführlich mit dem Thema befaßt. Er weist in seinem Buch Einzelheiten nach, die selbst damaligen Trägern dieser Uniform heute nicht mehr genau erinnerlich sind. Im Einsatz wurde nicht danach gefragt. Es wurden Stücke getragen, die praktisch und vor allem verfügbar waren.

In vorliegender Zusammenfassung werden nicht nur Form, Schnitt und Aussehen jedes Einzelstückes gezeigt, es wird auch das dafür verwendete Material und seine Verabeitung genau beschrieben, getrennt in Ausführungen für Führer, Unterführer und Mannschaften.

Nicht nur die Panzermänner, die diese Uniformen stolz einst trugen, danken dem Verfasser für diese historische Dokumentation in Wort und Bild. Es ist vielmehr ein Nachschlagewerk auf speziellem Gebiet für alle, die sich militärwissenschaftlich mit solchen Themen befassen.

Hans Siegel
Bad Teinach, den 4. Juli 1992

Ritterkreuzträger / Knight's Cross Holder HANS SIEGEL
SS-Sturmbannführer und Major der Waffen-*SS*
Commander 8./ II *SS*-Panzer Regiment 12
SS Panzer Division „Hitlerjugend"

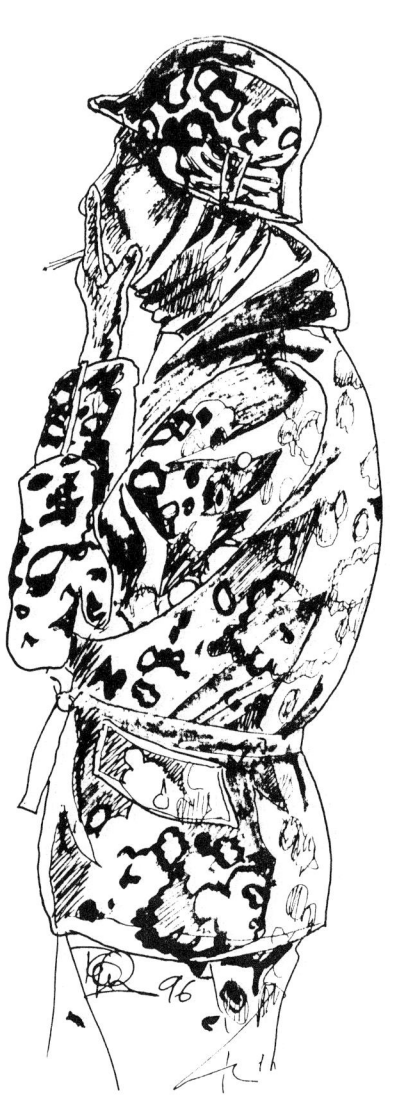

This ᛋᛋ-Uscha. has been awarded the Iron Cross First Class, the Tank Assault Badge, the Badge for the Single-Handed Destruction of a Tank in Silver and a Wound Badge.

Der alte Hase
The ⚡⚡ Panzer Regiment 1942 - 1945

Between the summer of 1942 and May of 1945, the panzer battalions and regiments of the Waffen-⚡⚡ were formed, committed to combat, and annihilated, leaving their mark in military history. ⚡⚡ panzer regiments were composed of two battalions (Abteilungen), each with four Kompanies of 17 to 22 tanks. Usually, the I. Abteilung was equipped with the newer, up-gunned tanks while the II. Abteilung used the older models. Although each Abteilung had its own headquarters and support company, overall command centered at the regimental headquarters company. A maintenance company serviced the entire regiment. The strength of an ⚡⚡ panzer regiment fluctuated between 1,200 to 2,000 troops, depending on leave and combat losses.

Der alte Hase
Understanding Waffen-ᛋᛋ Ranks and Rank Insignia

Waffen-ᛋᛋ rank titles evolved from the Allgemeine-ᛋᛋ and the ᛋᛋ-Verfugungstruppe. Depending on the rank and uniform, the individual rank was displayed on the uniform by different types of collar, shoulder, and sleeve insignia.

During the war the lengthy Waffen-ᛋᛋ ranks were often abbreviated to save time and space (This book makes use of these correct, wartime abbreviations).

In February 1943, a regulation was written which gave a branch of service prefix to the lower enlisted rank titles. In an ᛋᛋ-Panzer Regiment these rank titles would be ᛋᛋ-Panzerschütze and ᛋᛋ-Panzeroberschütze.

As in most armies, the Waffen-ᛋᛋ classified the four groups of rank as follows: enlisted, non-commissioned officers, officers, and general officers. (An individual's rank usually determined type and quality of insignia.) Usually, the highest rank found within an ᛋᛋ-Panzer Regiment was ᛋᛋ-Obersturmbannführer.

As in the German Army, the Waffen-ᛋᛋ had the duty position of „Der Spieß." This rank is compareable to the American company level "First Sergeant." Any NCO in the Waffen-ᛋᛋ could hold this position. The Spieß wore two rows of 9mm NCO tresse spaced 5mm apart and 13cm above each sleeve cuff. The Spieß often carried his orders and report book tucked into his uniform between the second and third buttons of the tunic.

Waffen-ᛋᛋ NCO and Officer Candidate Insignia

NCO candidates who had enlisted for more than twelve years of service wore a single slip-on slide of 9mm NCO tresse on both shoulder boards. If a soldier enlisted for less than twelve years, he wore either a 1.5 mm aluminum twist cord or a cord in the color of his branch of service on both shoulder boards. ᛋᛋ Officer candidates wore two slip-on slides of 9mm NCO tresse on their shoulder boards.

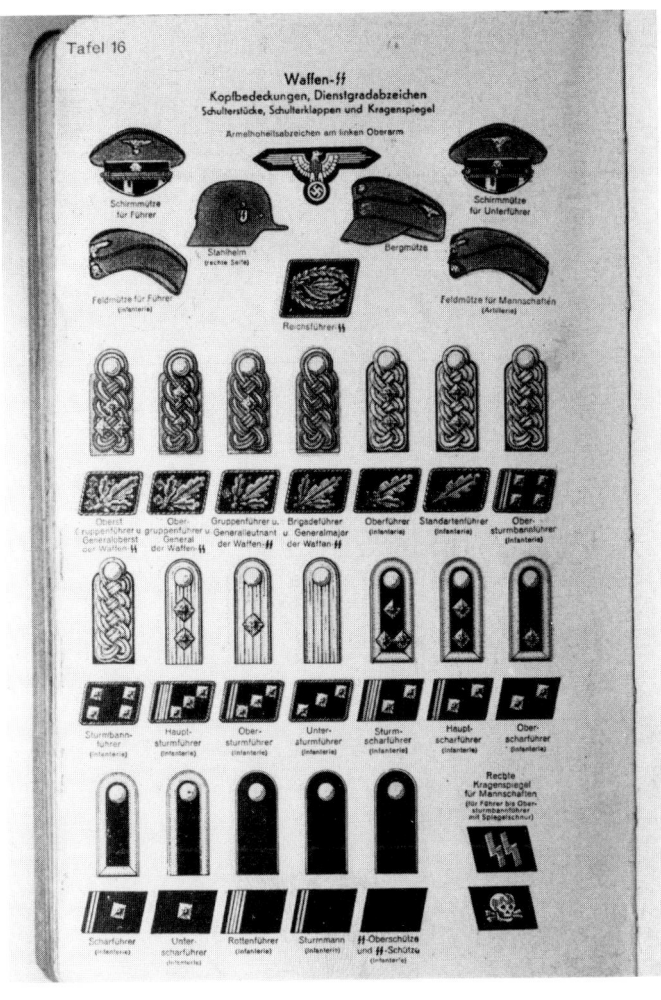

This Waffen-SS table of rank insignia originates from a 1943 „Soldatenfreund" (Soldier's Friend), a pocket book with calendar usually issued to new recruits.

A first winter survivor of the L⚡⚡AH wears a piped tunic.

Chapter One

Waffen-*SS* Panzer Uniforms

This *SS*-Unterscharführer wears a black shirt with his service jacket. A veteran of the first winter in Russia, he has also earned the Iron Cross Second Class, the Panzer Assault Badge, and the Wound Badge in Silver.

The Waffen-ϟϟ Panzer Service Jacket

The Waffen-ϟϟ Panzer Service Jacket differed from its German Army counterpart because it featured shorter, rounder lapels and collar. The double-breasted front of the jacket buttoned vertically, not at a right slant like the Army style. Four black, compressed-fiber, ceramic, or steinnus (hardened wood) buttons of 21-23mm in diameter closed the jacket front. The right side of the jacket front tucked behind, and was secured to, the left side by two 14mm buttons which fastened to two loops made of the same material as the jacket lining. In cold weather, it was possible to button the jacket to the throat using two additional 14mm buttons and a metal hook and eye sewn into the collar. The fit of the cuff could be adjusted with two more 14mm buttons positioned on the lower sleeve.

The Panzer Service Jacket was partially lined with linen in the early jackets and later with artificial silk. The color of the lining ran from shades of light brown, to gray, and to black. Two pockets were incorporated into the lining along with four adjustment tapes for a close fit. Two reinforced mounting tapes for the cartridge belt support hooks were sewn directly into the lining. These mounting tapes were often sewn down as the practice of wearing belt hooks with this jacket was not only unpopular but defeated the purpose of a snag-free uniform for wear within the confines of an armored vehicle. Size and condition codes were usually stamped on the inside left breast lining panel. The sizing was identical to that used by the army (see *SOLDAT* Volumes I, II, & III for details). The contractor numbers, or the ϟϟ-BW (Beschafungswerk) stamps, were either in this area or on the inside of either of the two pockets. A small loop was sewn into the lower, inside seam of the collar so that the jacket could be hung without using a hanger.

Period photos show individual ϟϟ men wearing pink, artificial-silk piping around the edge of their jacket collar, collar insignia, or both. This unofficial practice does not seem to have been influenced by the German Army's decision to discontinue piping on panzer jackets in mid-1942. This smart-looking addition was added to the jacket by home front or unit tailors. The practice was in total disregard to an order issued by Reichsführer Himmler in November 1940, which limited the wearing of service branch color to shoulder boards and overseas caps. Officers often substituted pink piping for the aluminum twist cord around their collar and collar insignia.

The Waffen-*ϟϟ* Panzer Service Jacket. This jacket features a tan-colored, partial linen lining (for more details of the jacket lining, see the Waffen-*ϟϟ* Field Gray Armored Service Jacket).

ϟϟ-Ustuf. Jeran, commander of the 3rd Platoon 8./III Abt. *ϟϟ* Panzer Rgt 12 „Hitlerjugend," wearing the Waffen-*ϟϟ* Panzer Service Jacket with Officers Brocade Belt and Buckle. To his left is *ϟϟ*-Hscha. Ernst Drebert of the 4th platoon wears the Naval Foul Weather Jacket. „Der "Spieß" wears a converted post-1940 production Army Model 1936 Service Tunic with Panzer Field Cap.

This soldier's machine-embroidered, runic collar insignia has the unofficial pink-colored, artificial-silk piping sewn around the edge.

This ₷₷-Uscha. has pink, artificial silk piping sewn around the collar and collar insignia of his Waffen-₷₷ Panzer Service Jacket. The piping was added by the company tailor and sewn underneath as opposed to into the collar, causing a slight ripple in the cloth. A metal cap skull takes the place of the more usual machine-woven insignia on the field cap.

⚡-Sturmbannführer Tychsen, commander of the ⚡-Panzer Rgt. 2, in the cupola of his command Panzer III. He is wearing the Waffen-⚡ Panzer Service Uniform with aluminum twist cord around the edging the collar.

Members of 5./II Abt. *H*-Panzer Rgt. 2 — „Das Reich." The officer standing in the center of the group deliberately removed the small Panzer IV pin from his tank destruction badge to prevent it from snagging things within the confines of his tank.

The Waffen-⚡⚡ Panzer Service Trouser

The Waffen-⚡⚡ Panzer Service Trouser was worn with the panzer service jacket. Made of the same black woolen cloth, the service trouser style originated from ski trousers found on the German ski slopes in the 1930s. One of the trouser's unique identifying characteristics was the radical inward leg taper just above the ankle. The cuff was split on the outside to allow easy passage of the foot. Sewn onto the cuff at each side of the split was a cloth tape that allowed the soldier a snug fit inside the boot top.

The trouser had side pockets that closed with button-down flaps. The flaps, set at a slight angle, varied in the number of closing buttons. Waffen-⚡⚡ design specifications called for the use of two buttons, but one-button flaps were normal. The trouser also incorporated one or two hip pockets, with or without flaps. This feature, like the presence or absence of belt loops or watch pockets, depended on the manufacturer.

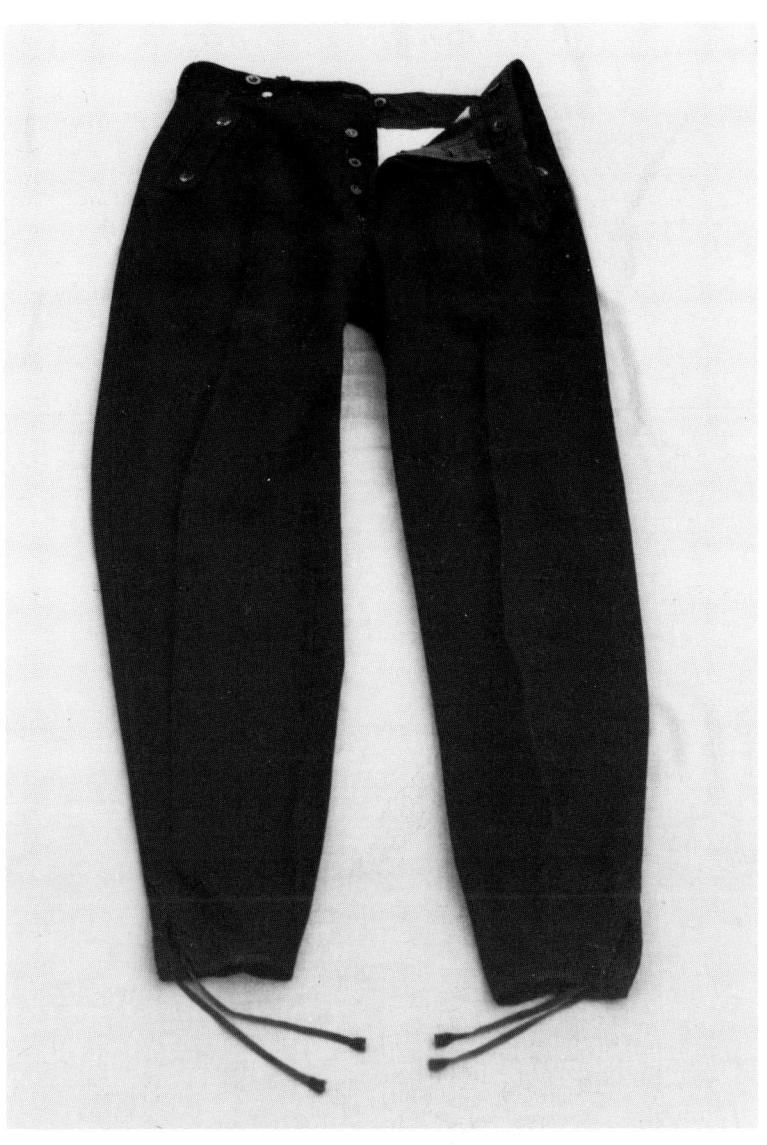

The Waffen-*SS* Panzer Service Trouser with double button, sidepocket, flaps.

The Waffen-⚡⚡ Field Gray Panzer Service Uniform

The Waffen-⚡⚡ Field Gray Panzer Uniform Jacket and Trousers were cut identically to the black Panzer Service Uniform. Worn predominantly by members of the assault artillery, or Sturmgeschütz, the jacket often had red branch piping sewn around the collar insignia and collars. In one major deviation from the standard demonstration of rank, NCOs of the "L⚡⚡AH" Sturmgeschütz Abteilung 1 sewed tresse around the collar edge. This tresse was a practice not observed by other ⚡⚡ armored or assault artillery formations.

This ⚡⚡-Sturmmann wears the Peaked Field Cap for NCOs and a civilian shirt with his uniform.

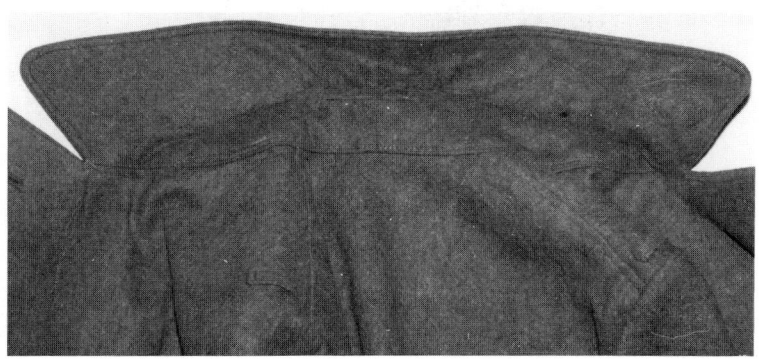

The front view of the Waffen-*SS* Field Gray Panzer Service Jacket. (Oregon National Guard Museum [ONGM]).

Details of the collar construction (ONGM).

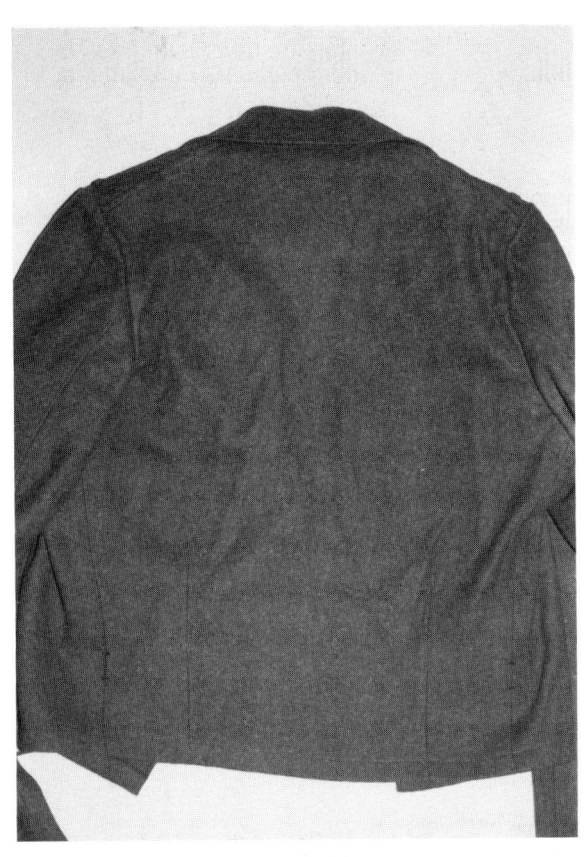

The rear view of the jacket (ONGM).

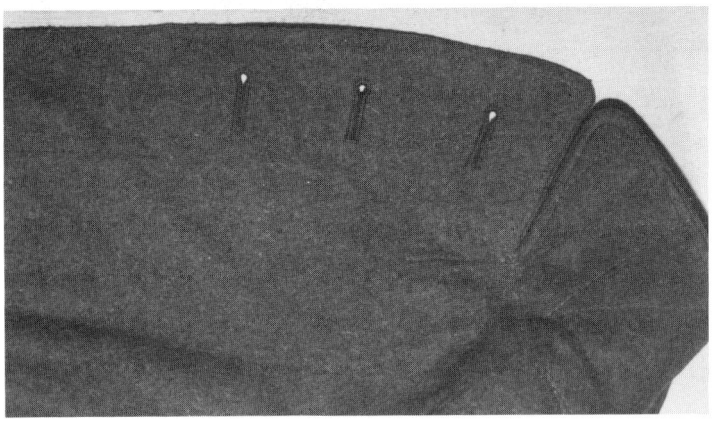

Details of the collar and exposed buttonholes on the left lapel (ONGM).

Details of the sleeve cuff and adjustment buttons (ONGM).

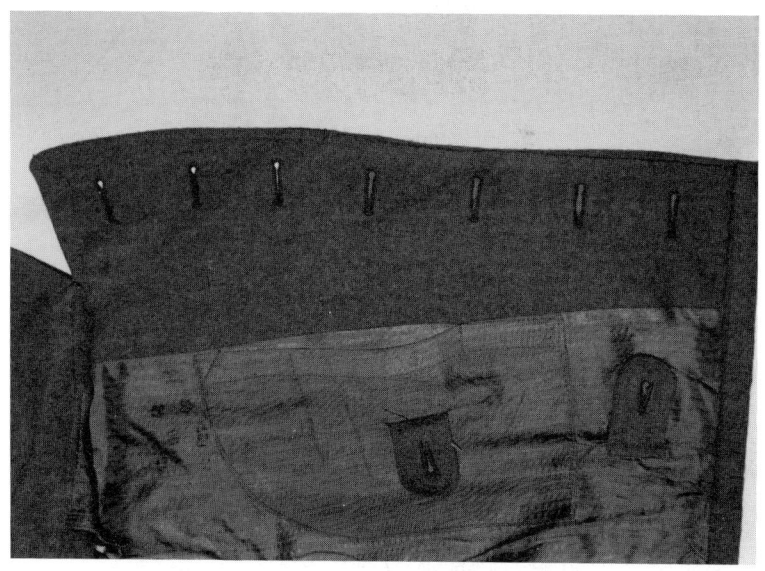

Details of the interior left side of the jacket (ONGM).

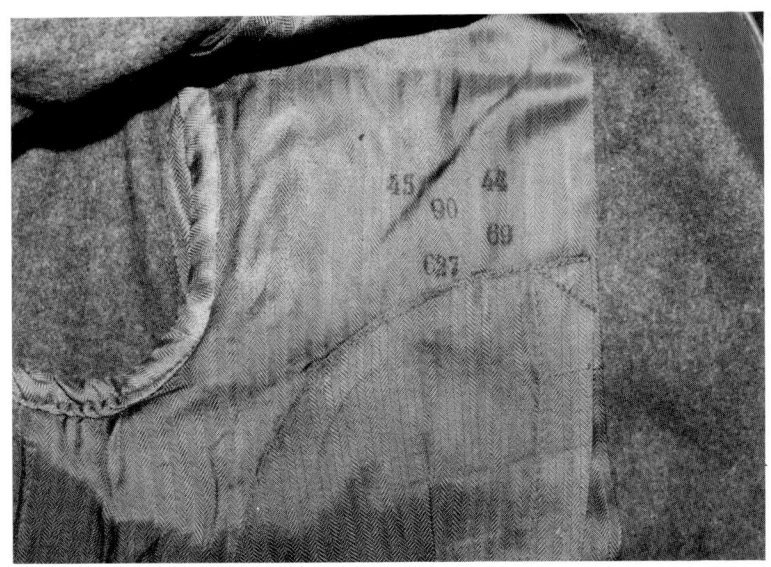

Interior markings (ONGM).

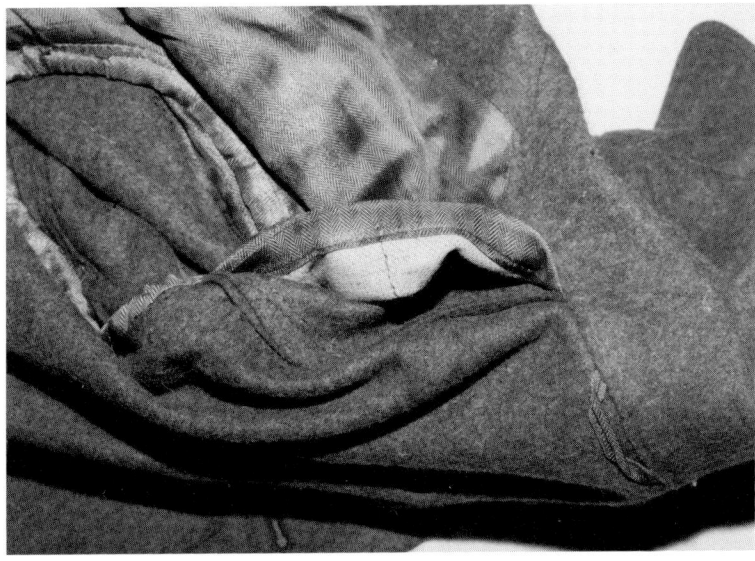

The inside of the interior pocket, showing the reverse of the herringbone material, artificial silk lining, and the collar loop for hanging the jacket.

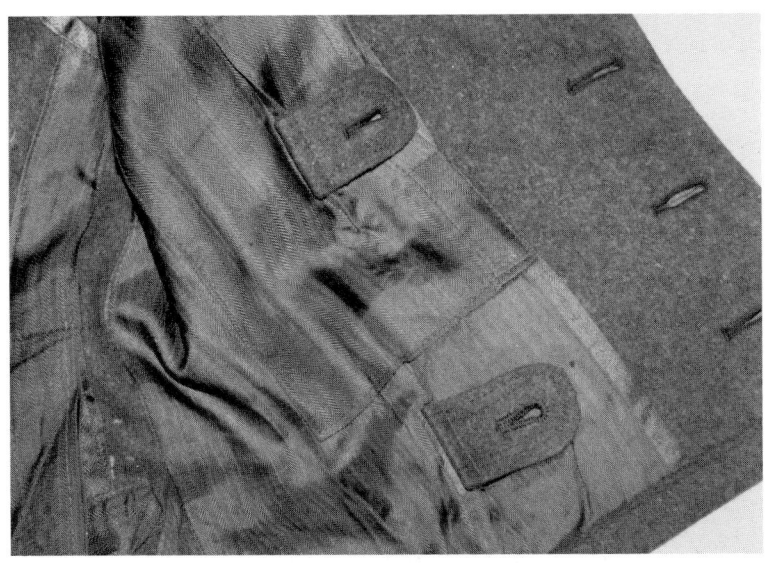

These tabs held the end of the right jacket panel in place.

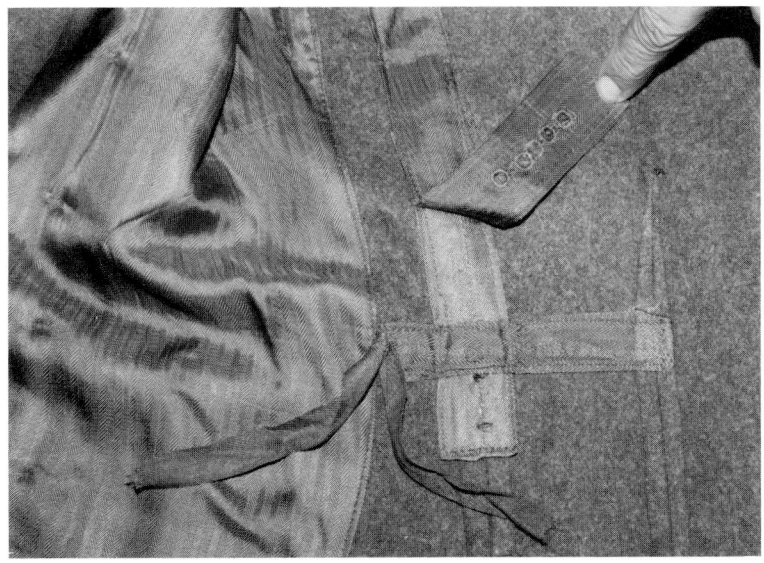

Size adjustment tapes and reinforced mounting tapes for the cartridge belt support hook (ONGM).

The ✠-Sturmmann wears red cord around his collar insignia.
His jacket has a variation in the narrow cut of the lapel and collar.

This "L⚡⚡AH" Rottenführer provides an excellent display of insignia and awards.

The German Army Artillerie School in Juterbog, May 1940. Members of the "LAH" Assault Gun Abt. wear the old-pattern field caps. The NCOs on the gun mantels both wear tresse on their collars. The ⚡⚡-Uscha. on the gun mantel of the Sturmgeschütz III on the right is Michael Wittmann. The officer in front is Knight's Cross holder Karl Rettlinger.

Just having received the Iron Cross 2nd Class, this ⚡⚡-Sturmmann poses with a polka-dot scarf and M43 Field Cap with metal insignia.

The Machine-Embroidered Sleeve Eagle shown as applied in the factory (ONGM).

-25-

A regulation-looking photo of this ᛋᛋ-Uscha., with the small exception of the metal eagle on the side of his single-button, M43 Field Cap.

The Waffen-⚡⚡ Issue Shirt and Necktie

During periods of warm weather, the commander could authorize the wearing of the shirt without the service jacket or necktie. The tie was black and made of artificial silk. The issue shirt came in two styles, the difference being with or without breast pockets. Shirts with pockets came with or without pocket pleats. Buttoning down to the navel, the shirt had to be pulled over the head for wear. The front, cuffs, and pockets were usually closed with pressed paper or metal buttons. Color of the issue shirt varied from shades of beige, brown, gray, green, and black. The most common form of insignia worn on the shirt were slip-on style shoulder boards.

On occasion soldiers would wear their awards on the shirt. Knight's Cross holders would wear this neck decoration without the tie.

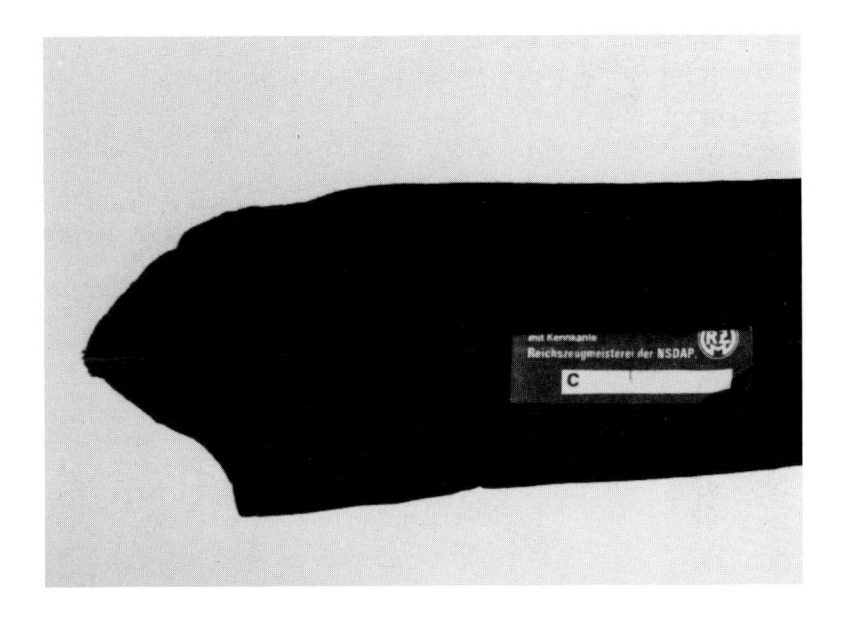

The artificial silk, Waffen-⚡⚡ Necktie with printed RZM Tag.

This ᛋᛋ-Unterscharführer of ᛋᛋ-Panzer Regiment 1 wears the Waffen-ᛋᛋ Issue Shirt with pocket pleats.

The Waffen-ℋ Belt Buckles

All ranks within the Waffen-ℋ were issued belt buckles bearing an eagle and the motto of the ℋ, „Meine Ehre heißt Treue" ("My Honor is Loyalty"), which was bestowed on November 9, 1931. There are two distinct patterns of belt buckles: enlisted and officer. Both were introduced in 1932 and remained unchanged throughout the war. Buckles were manufactured in the following manner:

- ✠Stamped Nickel - This type of buckle was produced predominantly before the beginning of the war. The buckle was of good quality metal and needed no additional plating or finish.
- ✠Stamped Steel - This type of buckle was very durable and was finished in what was known as "new silver finish," which was a form of zinc plating.
- ✠Die Cast Aluminum - This type of buckle was easy to produce but wore out quickly because of the soft nature of the material. The color of the metal was acceptable, but it was not plated.
- ✠Stamped "War Metal" - This type of buckle was produced from a zinc based metal with a high acidity level that causes the finish to oxidize and turn gray. These buckles were dipped in a silver "wash" or painted field gray or olive green. This was the only form of buckle production used for enlisted buckles.

This enlisted, 1932-pattern aluminum belt buckle still retains its original RZM Control Tag.

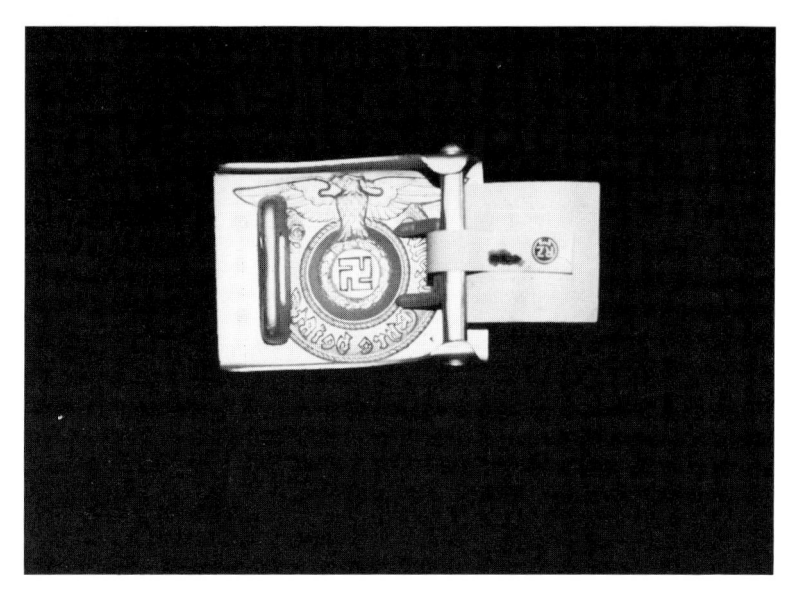

The reverse of the aluminum buckle showing the two-prong hook and RZM Tag.

The Officers 1932 pattern belt and buckle (Newman.)

Der alte Hase
Officers Belt and Buckle

Waffen-⚡⚡ officers would often wear the two-pronged, open-faced belt and buckle worn by German Army officers. On occasion ⚡⚡ officers would wear high quality Polish or Russian officer belts and buckles. This unofficial wear was very 'chic' and saved the more elaborate ⚡⚡ buckle from daily wear and tear.

The reverse showing the hook and manufacture stampings (Newman.)

-31-

A enlisted, stamped "War Metal" pattern belt buckle (Heinz.)

The reverse of this stamped "War Metal" belt buckle shows the fading of the silver "wash" and the 1943 control number (Heinz.)

The Waffen-⚡⚡ Leather Belts

The Waffen-⚡⚡ used leather belts of 4.4 or 4.5 cm in width. The cartridge belt had a metal hook sewn into the left end and a leather adjustment strap sewn into the right. By using pairs of holes punched into this strap, the fit of the belt could be adjusted, accommodating the soldier's waist size and equipment load. Cartridge belts produced later in the war omitted this strap, with the holes punched directly into the belt. The Waffen-⚡⚡ also used pressed paper belts introduced as another late war economy measure. Officers' belts had a buckle retainer sewn into the left end with the same adjustment strap sewn into the left.

Although most Waffen-⚡⚡ belts bore the same markings as their German Army counterparts, some belts can be observed with small ⚡⚡ runes and/or RZM stamped into the metal hook or leather of the belt. Some belts had large RZM ink stamps printed on the inside of the belt.

A late-war cartridge belt with the adjustment holes punched directly into the belt.

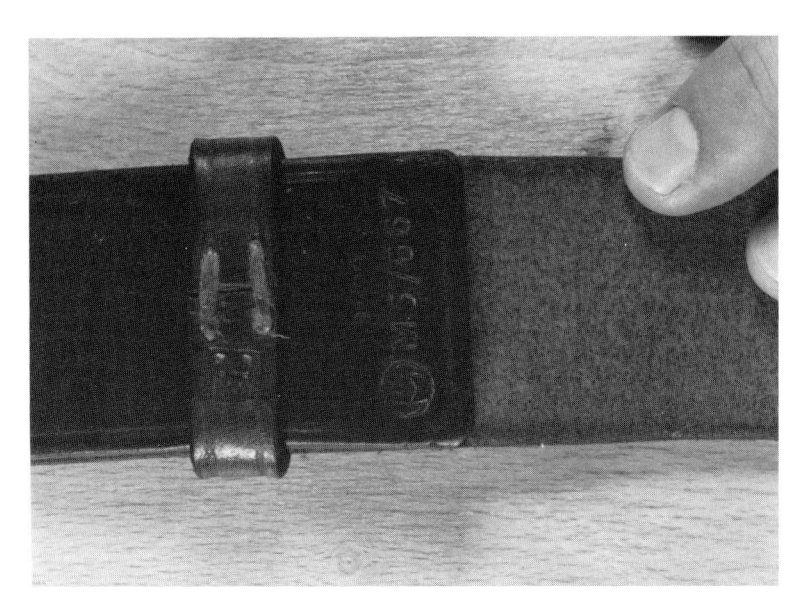

An officer's leather belt with RZM acceptance marks (Newman.)

Knight's Cross holder ⚡⚡-Unterscharführer Johann Thaler wears the Waffen-⚡⚡ Herringbone Twill Panzer Service Uniform in Normandy, 1944. The ⚡⚡-Uscha. to his right is wearing an Army pattern field cap with ⚡⚡ insignia.

The Waffen-ᛋᛋ Herringbone Twill (HBT) Panzer Service Uniform

In August 1941 a new, two-piece, herringbone twill (Drillich) service uniform was issued to panzer crewmen. The uniform was intended for wear over the woolen service uniform for protection and camouflage, or on its own during hot weather. The uniform was identical in cut and style to the service uniform, and it was not reversible. The uniform was partially lined with HBT cloth and closed with gray green ceramic or glass buttons positioned identically to the wool uniform. Durable, light weight, and easily washable, the HBT uniform was very popular among the tank crews. The HBT uniform first appeared in the "reed green" color, then in the Fall Oak Leaf camouflage pattern. In March 1944, the uniform was issued in the new Small-Leaves-on-Ochre and Small-Leaves-on-Fields camouflage pattern printed on both HBT and linen drill. Both the "reed green" and the camouflage uniforms were highly susceptible to fading from sunlight and washing, which caused the colors to fluctuate.

Although the only authorized insignia for this uniform was the sleeve eagle and the camouflage rank insignia—which was sewn 5mm below it—the individual soldier often added other insignia and awards.

This Panzer Soldat wears the ᛋᛋ HBT Panzer Service uniform with a black wool M-43 cap. (Newman)

-35-

Two views of the interior of the Waffen-⚡⚡ Herringbone Twill Panzer Service Jacket. The off-white color of the unprinted linen is visible as is the pocket, adjusting tape, and partial liner. The small, buttonholed flap sewn to the pocket holds the inside of the jacket's front panel in place while it is buttoned.

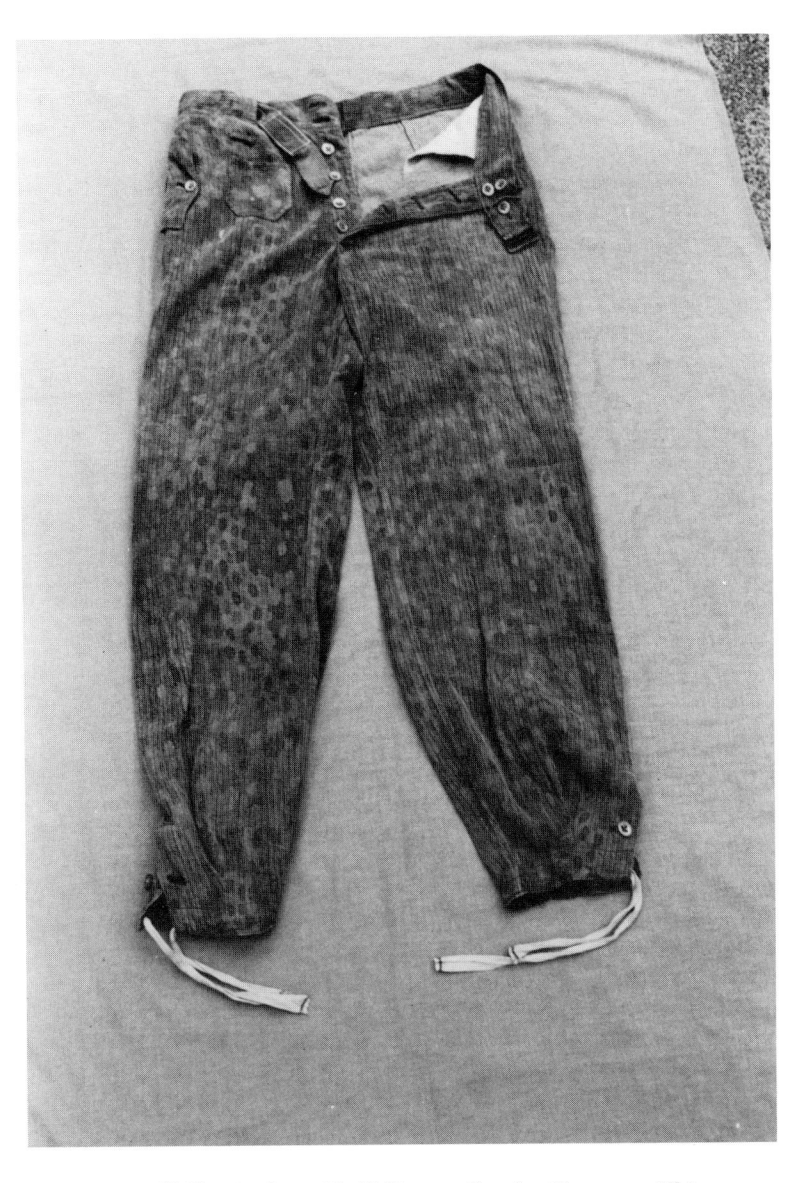

The Waffen-*SS* Herringbone Twill Panzer Service Trousers. This example has metal buttons.

The Waffen-⚡⚡ Reversible Camouflage Panzer Overall

First issued in early spring of 1943, the Waffen-⚡⚡ Reversible Camouflage Panzer Overall was probably the most practical uniform made for the tankers of the Waffen-⚡⚡. The overall was made of light-weight, tightly woven, water-repellent drill. Two large patch pockets were on both sides of the breast and an access flap was on each hip. The overall was closed by six 22 - 23mm black, gray-green, or tan bakelite plastic, four-holed buttons. On occasion, some overalls were fitted fully, or in part, with the standard pebbled metal buttons. The camouflage pattern was printed on both sides of the cloth, spring/summer on the predominant side. The overall was only printed in the following camouflage patterns: Plane Tree, Plane Tree / Oakleaf Combination, and Oakleaf.

The overall was issued without insignia; however, sleeve eagles, shoulder boards, or camouflage rank insignia were often added.

A Waffen-⚡⚡ tank commander wearing the reversible camouflage overall.

During a smoke break somewhere in Russia, these Panzer IV crewmen pose wearing the Plane Tree/Oakleaf Combination or Oakleaf pattern reversible camouflage overall.

This Panzer IV crew from the 6./II Abt. ⚡⚡-Panzer Rgt. 2 „Das Reich" are wearing the reversible camouflage overall in the Plane Tree / Oakleaf Combination or Oakleaf pattern. All but one wears the Leather Marching Boot.

The Waffen-⚡⚡ Reversible Winter Panzer Overall

During the winter of 1942 - 1943, some ⚡⚡-Panzer Regiments, certainly ⚡⚡-Panzer Rgt. 1, were issued a reversible winter overall. The overall was made of two layers of cloth, white and gray, and were cut identically to the reversible camouflage overall. As the overall was not insulated, it required the wearing of additional clothing to retain body heat. This additional clothing made getting in and out of the overall very difficult, especially problematic when defecating in a Russian snow bank. It was not as popular with tankers as the reversible, camouflage model; crewmen struggled to acquire the two-piece winter anorak and trouser used by Waffen-⚡⚡ troops.

Hans Siegel, then serving as an ⚡⚡ Obersturmführer in the L⚡⚡AH assault gun battalion, wears the reversible winter overall. He is setting a small demolition charge to destroy a captured Russian antitank gun.

-40-

The Italian Camouflage and Naval Foul Weather Uniforms

After the capitulation of Fascist Italy, liberated stocks of Italian camouflage material were tailored into uniforms and field caps of varied styles. The predominant feature found on the uniforms were large patch pockets. As with all other camouflage uniforms, the rank insignia for camouflaged uniforms was worn on the left sleeve, or sometimes on both.

The disarmament of the Italian armed forces also rendered large stocks of German-made, black leather naval, foul-weather uniforms free for reissue. Due to the high loss rate at sea, the uniforms were not required by the Kriegsmarine; they were issued to the II. Abteilung of ⚡-Panzer Rgt. 12, to some extent to ⚡-Regiment 1, and ⚡-Schwere Panzer Abteilung 103 (503). The intent was to provide the tankers with a uniform that would provide protection against an onboard fire.

There were two types of foul weather jackets, the difference being only in collar style. The first style featured a normal style collar, and the second a small stand-up style collar that did not fold down. When worn with the latter, the collar of the panzer service jacket would protrude outside, showing the runic and rank collar insignia. The only items worn on the jacket were shoulder boards and, on occasion, decorations.

This enlargement shows the eagle and large "M" Marine acceptance mark stamped into the front of the leather trouser.

This ϟϟ-Unterscharführer is wearing the complete Naval Foul Weather Uniform.

The Naval Foul Weather Jacket lining of dark gray wool.

A rear view of the leather Naval Foul weather Uniform. The sleeve cuff can be closed with an adjustment strap.

Details of the Naval Foul Weather Trousers showing the watch pocket, buttons for suspenders, manufacturer's label, and light gray, artificial silk lining.

Shown during the Normandy battles of 1944, ⚡⚡-Obersturmführer Herbert Hofler, Executive Officer of the 8./II Abt. ⚡⚡-Panzer Rgt. 12 „Hitlerjugend," wears this two-piece combat uniform made of Italian Army camouflage material.

Waffen-⚡⚡ Rank and their equivalents

American Rank Equivalent	Waffen-⚡⚡ and German Army Rank	Sleeve Rank Insignia
Lieutenant Colonel	Obersturmbannführer (Ostubaf.) Oberstleutnant	
Major	Sturmbannführer (Stubf.) Major	
Captain	Hauptsturmführer (Hstuf.) Hauptmann	
First Lieutenant	Obersturmführer (Ostuf.) Oberleutnant	
Second Lieutenant	Untersturmführer (Ustuf.) Leutnant	
Sergeant Major	Sturmscharführer (Stuscha.) Hauptfeldwebel	
Master Sergeant	Hauptscharführer (Hscha.) Oberfeldwebel	
Technical Sergeant	Oberscharführer (Oscha.) Feldwebel	
Staff Sergeant	Scharführer (Scharf.) Unterfeldwebel	
Sergeant	Unterscharführer (Uscha.) Unteroffizier	
Corporal	Rottenführer (Rttf.) Obergefreiter	
Private First Class	Sturmann (Strm.) Gefreiter	
Private	Panzeroberschütze ——— Oberschütze	

-45-

"Frundsberg" ᛋᛋ-Sturmann wearing a Heer M-43 Cap.

Chapter II

Waffen-SS Panzer Headgear

Different types of headgear in wear by members of SS-Panzer Regiment 2. On the left, the EM - NCO Visor Cap with metal insignia. In the center, the Army Model 1938 Officers Field Cap with machine-woven insignia and pink soutache. On the right, the SS-Obersturmführer wears the new pattern, Waffen-SS pattern field cap with aluminum piping around the top flap.

Waffen-SS Field Cap, Old Pattern

In 1937 a black wool, overseas-style cap was introduced for wear with the black political uniform. The cap, known by the nickname „Schiffchen" due to its shape resembling a small, upside-down boat, was worn by armored troops well into 1943.

The insignia of the Waffen-SS Field Cap, Old Pattern consisted of a 20mm metal button embossed with the death's head. The button was first finished in copper, later in silver, and with the outbreak of war, in different shades of field gray. The Totenkopf button was either sewn or pinned to the cap. After the introduction of the machine-woven death's head, individual soldiers often replaced the button (For examples of this change, see the private photos in *Verweht sind die Spuren*; Osnabruck, Munin Verlag. 1979, pages 20, 54, and 116). A small, machine-embroidered eagle on a black wool triangular background was sewn to the left side of the cap's flap. The wear of a branch soutache was authorized from 1939 and 1942, but in many cases it was worn unofficially until the end of the war. Officers who possessed this cap often added aluminum piping around the edges of the flap.

The machine-embroidered eagle and metal button with embossed death's head used on the Waffen-SS Field Cap, Old Pattern.

Der alte Hase: Marking Headgear

Waffen-ℋ soldiers often marked their headgear for easy recognition by writing their name or initials inside the hat. Small, metal initial badges could be purchased and crimped to the sweatband. Cloth labels could be sewn in place or initials hand stitched into the hat.

The Waffen-ℋ Field Cap, New Pattern

Prior to January, 1940, Waffen-ℋ officers often purchased Army Model 1938 Officer's Field Caps and converted them for ℋ use by replacing all, or part, of the insignia. After the introduction of the new pattern Waffen-ℋ cap, officers were required to replace their Army caps. The new cap was introduced for enlisted issue in November 1940.

The new cap was cut in the same style as the Luftwaffe Field Cap and was in black wool for tank crewmen. Machine woven death's head and national eagle were sewn on the front of the cap. The insignia for the enlisted cap was woven in gray thread and in aluminum for the officer's cap. An inverted "V" of pink soutache was occasionally worn on the front of the cap.

Lernen durch Erfahrung

Soutache is a flat braid woven in a herringbone pattern. A length of this braid was positioned on the front of some ℋ field caps in an inverted "V," with its apex coming to a point above the death's head insignia. The bottom tails of the "V" were either sewn down in place on the cap's front or passed through tiny holes and sewn down behind the cap's flap. The official distance between the two ends was 9cm. In September of 1942, the wearing of branch-colored soutache officially ended.

Three examples of the enlisted, machine-woven cap eagle.

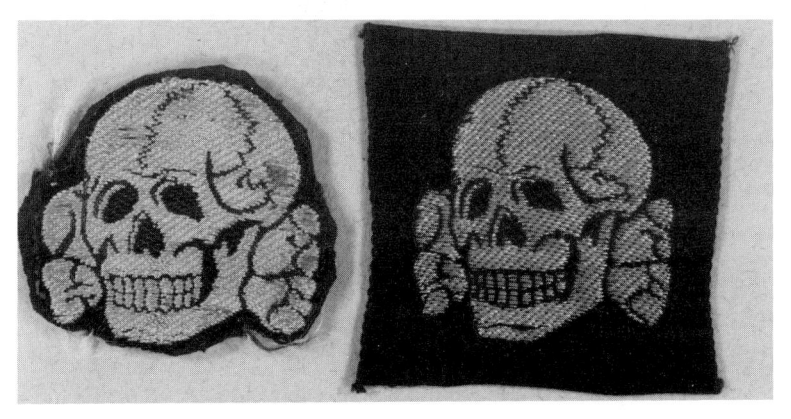

Enlisted and officer Totenkopf. The officer's skull on the right is woven in aluminum thread and is uncut for placement on a cap.

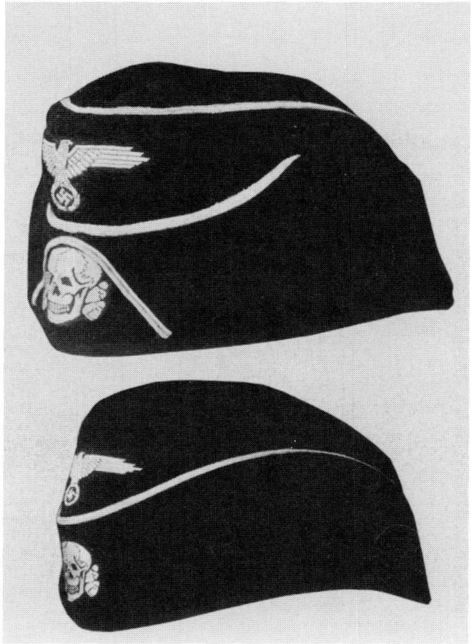

The Army M38 Officer's Field Cap modified for Waffen-ᛋᛋ use with the addition of insignia and pink soutache. Below, the Waffen-ᛋᛋ Officer's Field Cap, New Pattern.

The Waffen-ᛋᛋ Field Cap, Old Pattern as used originally by the ᛋᛋ-VT. Below, the Waffen-ᛋᛋ Field Cap, New Pattern.

SS-Hauptsturmführer Michael Wittmann wears the Waffen-*SS* Peaked Field Cap for NCOs.

The Waffen-⚡⚡ Peaked Uniform Cap

With the discontinuation of the black political uniform, a new Peaked Uniform Cap was introduced for wear by enlisted soldiers on leave or when wearing the "walking out" uniform. The new cap had a field gray top, black cloth band, and white piping. The visor was made of hard black fiber and the chin strap of black leather. The chin strap was constructed in two separate sections joined at the center by an elongated metal ring. Adjustment buckles were located at either end of the chin strap, which was fastened to the cap by two 12-13mm smooth, black buttons. Metal insignia was normally used on this cap.

Officers wore the Peaked Uniform Cap during duty whenever a steel helmet wasn't necessary. With the introduction of the officer's field cap in 1939, the peaked cap was used only on leave or when wearing the "walking out" uniform. The cap had a field gray top, black velvet band, and white piping. Officers above the rank of ⚡⚡-Standartenführer had aluminum piping. The regulation visor was of black fiber, but often soft leather was added unofficially. The chin strap was of twisted aluminum cords, with adjusting slides on either end. The strap was looped at either end and was secured to the cap by 12-13mm pebbled, aluminum buttons sewn or pinned in place. Metal insignia was normally used on this cap.

Lernen durch Erfahrung

The use of colored piping on Peaked Uniform Caps was only authorized between May and November 1940. At this time Reichsführer Himmler directed that all colored piping be discontinued on Waffen-⚡⚡ uniforms, with the exception of shoulder boards and the soutache found on the field cap. Many officers and NCOs disregarded this order and wore their branch-piped caps until the end of the war. The authorized color after November 1940 was white.

The Waffen-⚡⚡ Peaked Field Cap for NCOs

In 1938 a peaked cap was introduced for wear by NCOs while in the field. The cap had a soft, field gray cloth visor and top, black band, and white piping. The cap had no wire stiffener to keep the shape of the crown and peak, giving the cap a more "veteran" appearance. Individuals modified their cap's shape to their liking by pinching the peak to make it more prominent. No chin strap was worn with this cap.

The cap was originally intended for wear by NCOs only, but it was very popular with officers in the field. Many, who had at one time been NCOs, retained their caps. Unofficially, caps made with soft, black leather visors were worn at the front. The insignia worn on this cap was metal, machine woven, or a mixture. In rare instances the machine-embroidered eagle and skull originally designed for the discontinued Panzer beret found its way onto these caps.

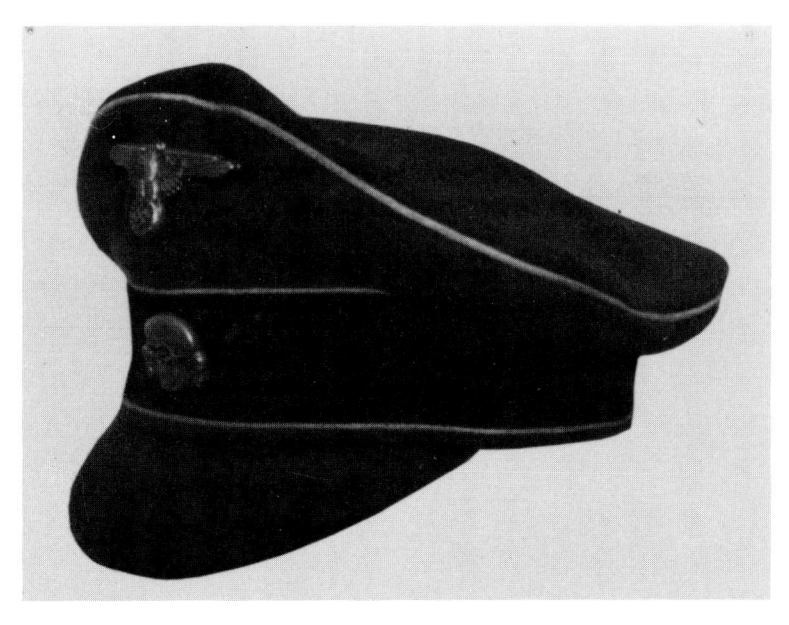

The Waffen-⚡⚡ Peaked Field Cap for NCOs with field gray, cloth visor.

The Waffen-⚡⚡ Enlisted Peaked Uniform Cap.

The Waffen-⚡⚡ Officer's Peaked Uniform Cap.

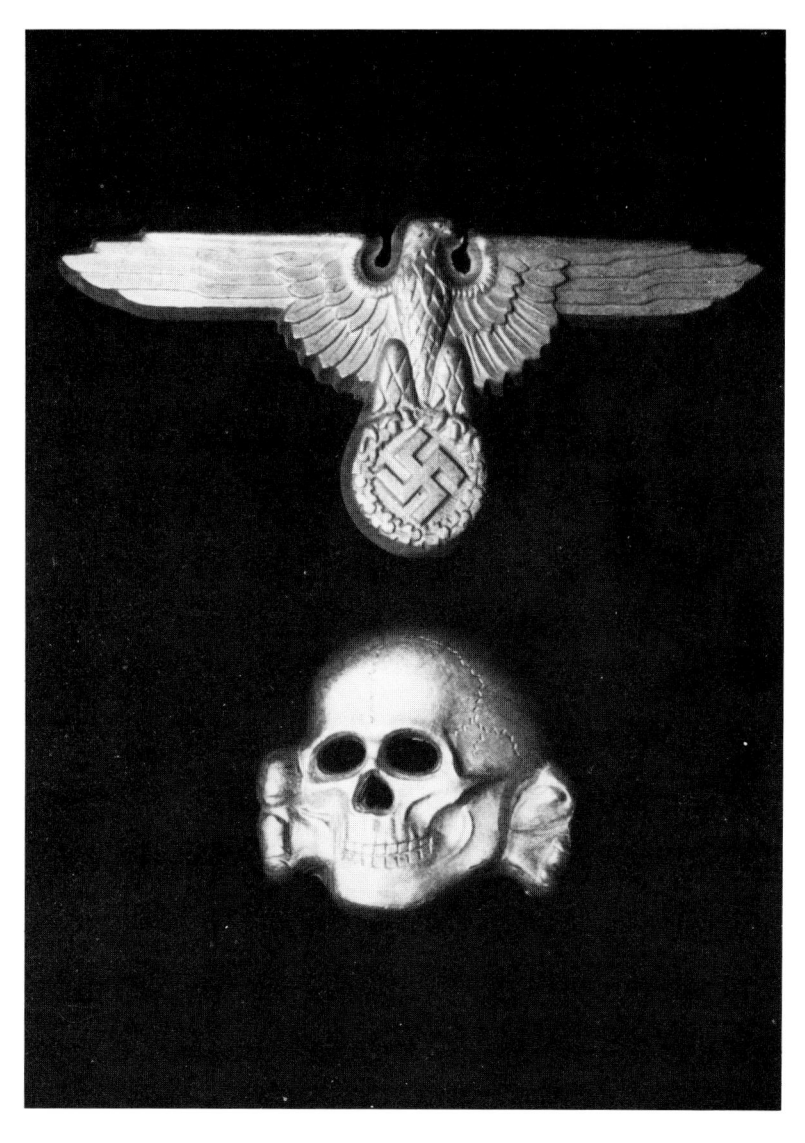

The front view of an aluminum example of the Waffen-*SS* Metal Insignia for Peaked Caps.

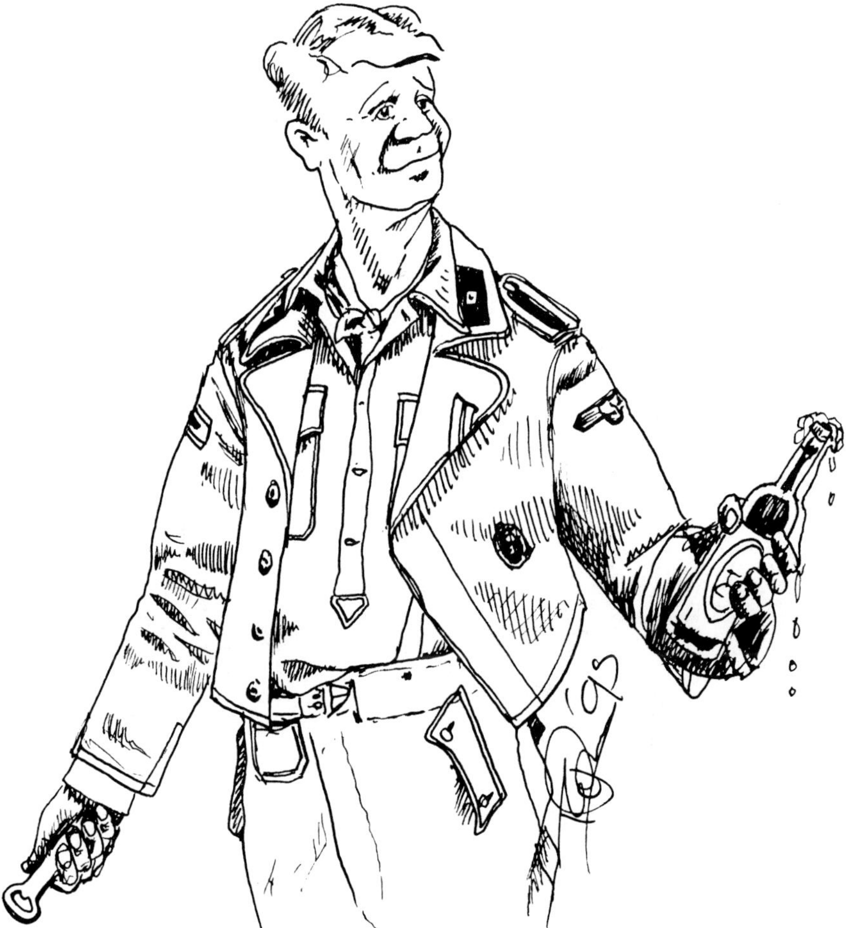

The Waffen-⚡⚡ Metal Insignia for Peaked Caps

Waffen-⚡⚡ Metal Insignia for Peaked Caps consisting of the national eagle and the Totenkopf were produced in a number of different metals. The earliest issues were silvered tin. As the war progressed, aluminum was used, and, as an economy measure, late war insignia were of „Kriegs metall" (a low quality zinc alloy, somewhat like pot metal.) All metal insignia was fastened to the cap with metal prongs.

The pre-1934 metal cap skulls were of a slightly larger size and were styled after the Prussian Life Hussar Regiments 1 and 2 cap badges. This early style can be observed on officers' caps as late as 1943.

Although the metal insignia was intended for use only on the peaked caps, its practical and simple application led to troops using the metal insignia on other types of headgear as well.

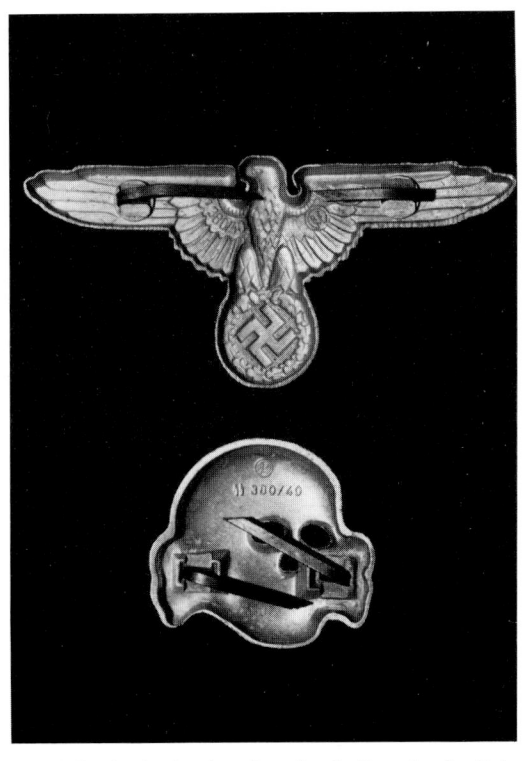

The rear view of the insignia showing the hollow back, flat attaching prongs and ⚡⚡ RZM marks.

The Waffen-ϟϟ Camouflage Field Cap

In May, 1942, Waffen-ϟϟ troops were initially issued a camouflage field cap made of tightly woven, semi-waterproof cloth. The first pattern of this cap had a short visor and was not reversible. The second pattern was reversible with the spring/summer side being predominant; the fall/winter side had the sewn-in sweat band and top seam. The first pattern caps had air vent holes radially-stitched, while the second pattern had field gray or green metal grommets. The air vent holes were located in pairs on both sides and near the top of cap.

Machine-woven eagles and skulls, identical in pattern to other field cap insignia, were made from dark green and brown thread. Although only authorized for about 15 days, these rare pieces of insignia were sewn to the center front of the cap, often in block form. Sewing the insignia in this manner and not following the exact shape of the design saved time and helped align the insignia to the same position on each side of the cap.

An example of a second pattern camouflage field cap with metal grommets.

The Waffen-⚡⚡ Model 1943 Field Cap and its Insignia

In 1943 a new field cap was introduced for use by the troops of the German Wehrmacht and the Waffen-⚡⚡. The cap style was derived from the Bergmütze issued to mountain troops. Unlike the older field cap, the new cap provided excellent protection from the elements with a large visor and fold-down flaps that could be brought down over the ears and under the chin. Early caps had two hidden loops sewn into the sides of the flap to enable the soldier to securely fasten the cap to his service uniform jacket or greatcoat shoulder boards. Due to its practical design and smart looks, the M43 Field Cap was well received by the troops.

Caps used by the armored troops were made of black wool and usually had an artificial silk liner. Officer's caps had aluminum piping sewn around the crown of the cap and normally featured insignia machine woven with aluminum thread. The arrangement of insignia could be in any of the following ways:

- ✠ Eagle and skull worn together centered on the front as seen on the field cap.
- ✠ The skull centered alone on the front and with the eagle being worn alone on the upper left side flap.
- ✠ The use of a trapezoid combination with both eagle and skull. This insignia was specifically designed for the M43 cap and was intended to standardize the appearance of the caps. This style of insignia was manufactured in machine embroidered and woven style, but only in the enlisted pattern.

Two machine-woven examples of the combination insignia which was used on the black wool, Waffen-*SS* Model 1943 Field Cap.

-61-

An early issue M43 Field Cap with two metal buttons and two-piece insignia. A late war issue M43 Field Cap with single bakelite button and one-piece combination insignia.

Chapter III:

Regimental Insignia of the Waffen-⚡⚡ Panzer Regiments

In Charkow, during the spring of 1943, ⚡⚡-Mann Joachim Glade wears a machine-embroidered „Adolf Hitler" cuff title and the slip-on LAH monogram on his shoulder boards. Even at this date, the old pattern ⚡⚡-VT field cap is still in use.

⚡⚡ *Panzer Regiment 1*
1. ⚡⚡ *Panzer Division*
„*Leibstandarte-*⚡⚡ *Adolf Hitler"*

All Waffen-⚡⚡ and Army pattern panzer jackets and field caps were worn during the regiment's formation period. Army style officers' field caps were worn quite often instead of the ⚡⚡ pattern, with full or partial ⚡⚡ insignia. In 1944, and up until the end of the war, Naval foul weather uniforms were issued in limited numbers.

The cuff title „Adolf Hitler," in Sutterlin script, was unique to this division and ⚡⚡-Panzer Regiment 1, as all other cuff titles were in Latin script.

The most common patterns of LAH cuff titles. From the top: enlisted machine embroidered, enlisted machine woven, and officer's machine woven.

Members wore a stylized LAH monogram on their shoulder board. There were three patterns of this monogram.

First, the slip-on monogram worn by those soldiers with the rank of ⚡-Unterscharführer and below. The LAH was embroidered in silver gray into a black loop. The better quality of these had a blanket stitch on each edge. A common practice was to cut out the monogram and sew it directly onto the shoulder board.

Second, NCOs wore machine-stamped, aluminum monograms secured to the shoulder board by 2-3 flat prongs. The prongs were very brittle and often broke off. The soldier would then simply sew them in place.

Third, officers wore monograms of gold-colored, white, or gray metal or copper colored metal.

Lernen durch Erfahrung

The slip-on was introduced in May 1940, which rules out the possibility of pink-piped shoulder boards with the LAH embroidered directly into the shoulder board.

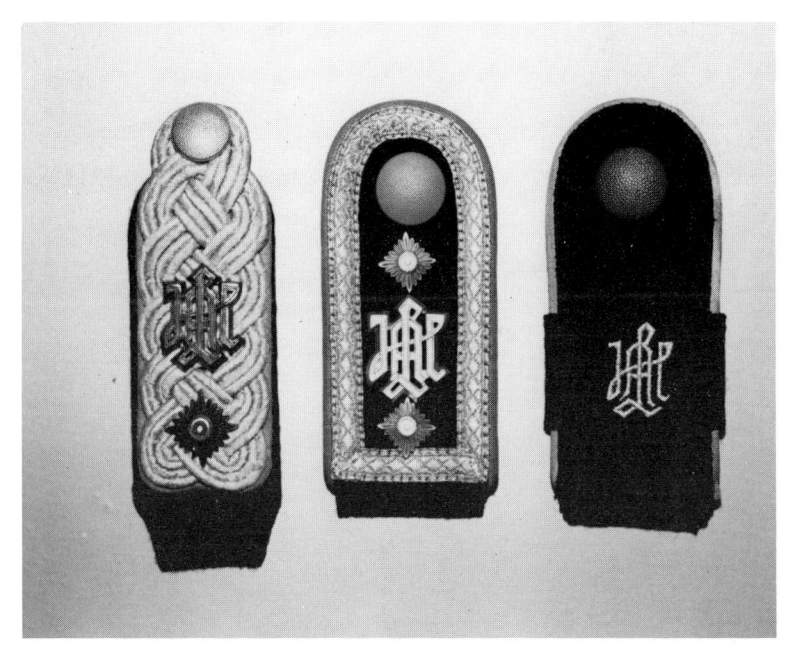

The three styles of LAH monograms.

Der alte Hase

Although often disregarded, an order issued in October 1943 by Reichsführer-*ᚼᚼ* Himmler forbid the wear of numbers on shoulder boards. In April 1944, a further order forbid the wearing of all unit monograms with the exception of the LAH, which was officially sanctioned for wear until the end of the war.

This L*ᚼᚼ*AH Sturmmann has sewn his LAH monogram, from the slip on, directly to his shoulder boards.

Details of the lower enlisted slip-on LAH monogram.

A fine example of a pink-piped ⚡⚡- Hauptscharführer shoulder board and machine-stamped LAH monogram. The pips are the smaller, 12mm size to compensate for the size of the monogram.

-67-

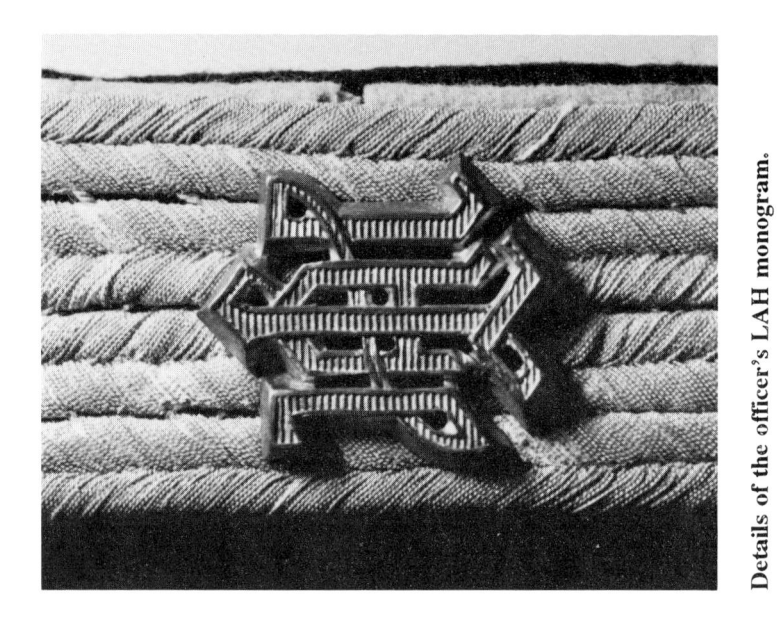

Details of the officer's LAH monogram.

Details of the NCO LAH monogram.

ᛋᛋ-Panzer Regiment 2
2. ᛋᛋ-Panzer Division „Das Reich"

Members of „Das Reich" wore all patterns of Waffen-ᛋᛋ uniforms and field caps. The divisional cuff title, „Das Reich," is in Latin letters. Members of the I. Abteilung occasionally wore the regimental number 2 on their shoulder board as well as pink piping around the uniform collar and collar insignia.

The enlisted, machine-woven „Das Reich" cuff title and ᛋᛋ-Obershcarführer shoulder board showing the unofficial addition of the regimental number 2.

⚡⚡-Hauptscharführer Fritz „Bello" Haupt, 6./II ⚡⚡-Panzer Regiment 2 wears a machine-embroidered „Das Reich" cuff title.

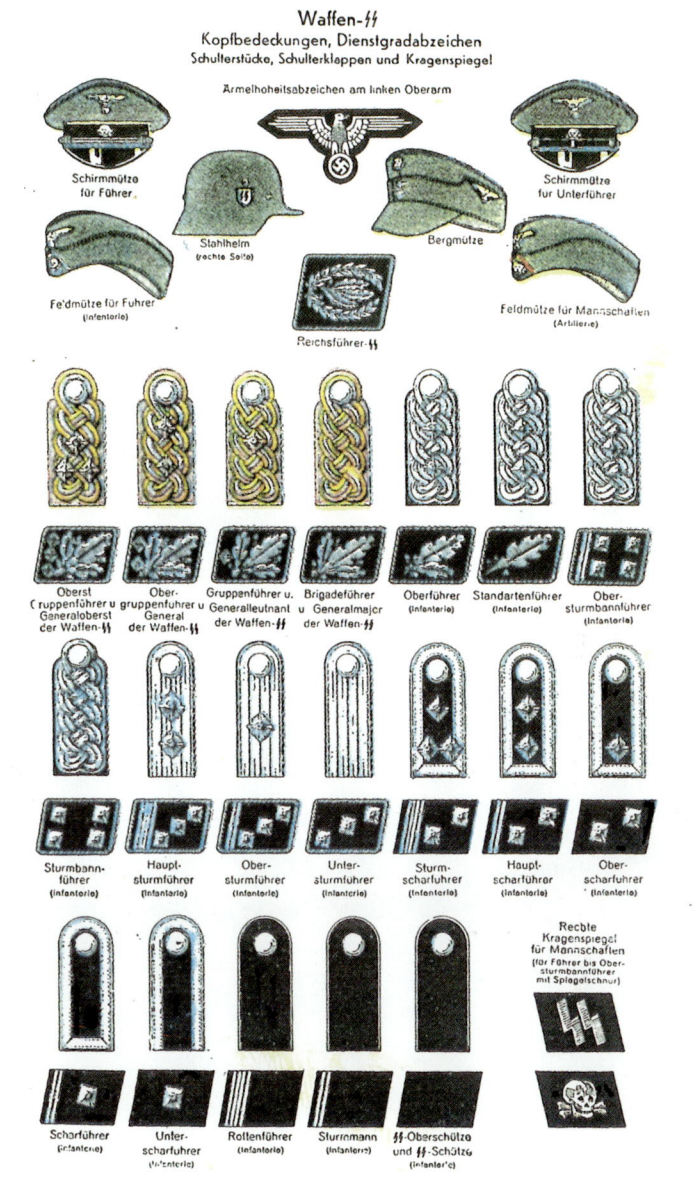

Ranks and headgear as shown in a private purchase soldier's manual.

This painting of an ◊-Unterscharführer from the ◊-Panzer Regiment 5 „Wiking" clearly shows the use of pink piping sewn around his collar and collar insignia.

The herringbone twill Panzer uniform

The black leather, Naval foul weather uniform.

An example of Italian camouflage

Two examples of coloration and fading on the "Reed Green" herringbone twill

Three examples and color variations of the rank insignia for camouflage uniforms.

An assorted mixture of Waffen-ᛋᛋ Panzer Regiment insignia and military awards.

Small Leaves on Fields printed on linen drill cloth.

Small Leaves on Ochere printed on herringbone twill cloth. (Newman)

Oak Leaf pattern printed in the Spring/Summer pattern.

Oak Leaf pattern printed in the Fall/Winter pattern.

Oak Leaf with Shadows pattern printed in the Spring/Summer pattern.

Oak Leaf with Shadows pattern printed in the Fall/Winter pattern.

Plane Tree and Oak Leaf Camouflage shown with ᛋᛋ fuel cans and 7.5 cm cannon round casing. (Newman)

The Plane Tree/Oak Leaf Combination, Spring/Summer top and Fall/Winter bottom, camouflage pattern.

⚡⚡-Panzer Regiment 3
3. ⚡⚡-Panzer Division „Totenkopf"

The men of the „Totenkopf" division wore all patterns of Waffen-⚡⚡ uniform and field caps. The insignia worn by the division's panzer regiment was unique and diverse in contrast to the other ⚡⚡-Panzer Regiments. This diversity was caused by the division's pre-war development of insignia. The pre-war Totenkopf collar insignia were in a vertical format. This format was due to the black, political uniform of the ⚡⚡-VT, which was worn open at the neck with shirt and tie, and the skull would then appear in a horizontal position.

When the division was being formed, matching, vertical skulls were worn on both sides of the collar in an attempt to match the German Army tradition of wearing identical collar insignia. The rank of the soldier was only displayed on the shoulder board, and, in cases of lower enlisted men, on the sleeve. Combat experience in Poland and France proved this arrangement of insignia to be impractical. Soldier's shoulder boards and sleeves were concealed under the camouflage smock!

In May 1940 a new order rendered the vertical/identical collar insignia obsolete. The rank insignia was to be worn on the left side of the collar like all other units. The same order also changed the positioning of the skull from vertical to horizontal, which was more uniform with the positioning of the ⚡⚡ Runic Collar Insignia. The new positioning was optically more appealing on the closed collar of the field gray tunic.

The divisional cuff title, in Latin letters, was worn by the regiment. Some members of the 1. ⚡⚡-Totenkopf Standarte „Oberbayern" continued to wear their old regimental "skull" cuff titles on their new panzer uniforms.

Vertical Skulls—The officer's hand embroidered, vertical collar insignia was introduced in 1937 and officially discontinued in May 1940. The enlisted, machine-embroidered, vertical collar insignia was introduced in 1939 and officially discontinued in May 1940. In spite of the May order and introduction of horizontal skulls, the vertical pattern continued to be worn until the end of the war as pairs or singularly on the right side, with the collar rank insignia on the left side.

-88-

Horizontal Skulls Facing Right—The officer's hand-embroidered collar insignia. This example is missing the 1.5mm aluminum twist cord. The enlisted collar insignia, machine embroidered in artificial silk. Although introduced in May 1940, horizontal skulls facing to the right are not as common as those facing to the left. Perhaps this variation was due to production from uncut stocks of the obsolete vertical pattern, or simply a variation. In some rare instances, and contrary to the 1940 regulation, they are seen worn on the left side of the collar as well as the right, forming a double- image, horizontal pair.

Horizontal Skulls Facing Left—The officer's hand embroidered collar insignia. This example is missing the 1.5mm aluminum twisted cord, which could indicate private purchase and wear by an NCO. The enlisted machine- embroidered collar insignia.

Horizontal Skulls Facing Left. The officer's machine-woven collar insignia. The enlisted machine-woven collar insignia. Both of these patterns were introduced in 1943 and face only to the left.

A private purchase cuff title in Gothic, hand-embroidered lettering (Heinz.)

Three cuff titles worn by members of the 3.*ϟϟ*-Panzer Division. The top two are the official regimental cuff title for the 1.*ϟϟ*-Totenkopf Standarte „Oberbayern." Both are officer patterns; the top is machine woven and the bottom hand embroidered. Below is the machine woven pattern worn by all ranks.

⚡⚡-Panzer Regiment 5
5. ⚡⚡-Panzer Division „Wiking"

„Wiking" division soldiers wore all Waffen-⚡⚡ patterns of uniform and field cap, commonly wearing pink piping on the collar and collar insignia.

The divisional cuff title was only produced officially in Latin lettering, but some individuals wore cuff titles, of unknown origin, lettered in Gothic style. The wearing of the regimental "5" on shoulder boards was widespread among NCOs and officers.

⚡⚡-Oscha. Hugo Ruf, a platoon leader in the 3. /I ⚡⚡-Panzer Regiment 5, wearing a machine- embroidered pattern „Wiking" cuff title. He was decorated with the Knights Cross on October 16, 1944.

Both of these cuff titles are machine woven. The top is for enlisted soldiers while the bottom is for officers. The shoulder board is a slip-on style for an ⱴ-Hauptscharführer and has had the "5" added unofficially.

-95-

⚡⚡-Panzer Regiment 9
9. ⚡⚡-Panzer Division „Hohenstaufen"
and
⚡⚡-Panzer Regiment 10
10. ⚡⚡-Panzer Division „Frundsberg"

Soldiers from the „Hohenstaufen" and „Frundsberg" divisions wore all patterns of Waffen-⚡⚡ uniforms and field caps. Often the members of both regiments added pink piping to their collars and collar insignia.

„Hohenstaufen"

According to a divisional order, the 9. ⚡⚡-Panzergrenadier Division received the title „Hohenstaufen" on March 19, 1943. The cuff titles were distributed the same day. With the arrival of enough Panzer V „Panther" tanks in October of that year, the division was upgraded to a Panzer Division on October 26, 1943. Members of ⚡⚡-Panzer Regiment 9 were entitled to wear the cuff title „Hohenstaufen" in Latin lettering. This cuff title was machine-woven in one pattern for all ranks.

The division name originates from the Hohenstaufen dynasty, a ruling German family, which held power from 1138 to 1254. The greatest emperor in the line was Frederick I, who was also known as Barbarrosa (Red Beard).

„Frundsberg"

All ranks of ⚡⚡-Panzer Regiment 10 wore the „Frundsberg" machine-woven cuff title in Latin letters. The final name of the division, prescribed by Adolf Hitler on October 3, 1943, became effective on November 20, 1943. The cuff title was distributed shortly thereafter.

The division name originates from a famous German knight named Georg von Frundsberg who lived form 1473 to 1528 and served the ruling Hapsburg family.

Machine woven in artificial silk, „Hohenstaufen" and „Frundsberg" cuff titles as worn by all ranks. A machine-woven variation of the „Hohenstaufen" cuff title exists with minor differences in the lettering detail as well as the letters "n" and "s" being connected at the bottom.

ᛋᛋ-Oscha. Josef Holte, Knight's Cross holder (posthumously), wears a machine-woven „Hohenstaufen" cuff title on his pink-piped panzer service uniform.

⚡⚡-Panzer Abteilung 11 „Hermann von Salza"
11. ⚡⚡-Freiwilligen Panzergrenadier Division „Nordland"

„Hermann von Salza" soldiers wore all of the Waffen-⚡⚡ patterns of uniforms and field caps. Conflicting accounts exist by veterans regarding the use of red piping around the collar and collar insignia worn on the Panzer Service Jacket. The color red was normally used only by artillery men or assault gun crewmen. The Abteilung had a large contigent of assault guns, which served as fillers for the shortage of tanks. Thus, this use of red is feasible.

Because of the high content of Nordic volunteers, the official divisional collar insignia was a sun wheel, which looks like a rounded-off swastika. In spite of this insignia, the members of the Panzer Abteilung wore the usual ⚡⚡ runic collar insignia.

Even though the Abteilung never reached the intended strength of a Panzer Regiment due to shortages in armor, it was issued a cuff title bearing the name „Hermann von Salza." Prior to this new cuff title issue, the Abteilung members wore the „Nordland" cuff title. ⚡⚡-Panzer Abteilung 11 was the only armored battalion to have been issued its own cuff title.

Hermann von Salza was founder and Grand Master of the powerful Teutonic order (Teutonic Knights). He lived from 1170 to 1239 and was a consultant and friend to Emperor Frederick II. He escorted the emperor on the crusade of 1228-29. Hermann von Salza also assisted Emperor Konrad I in suppressing the Prussians, which gave him the chance to establish the headquarters of the Teutonic order in Prussia.

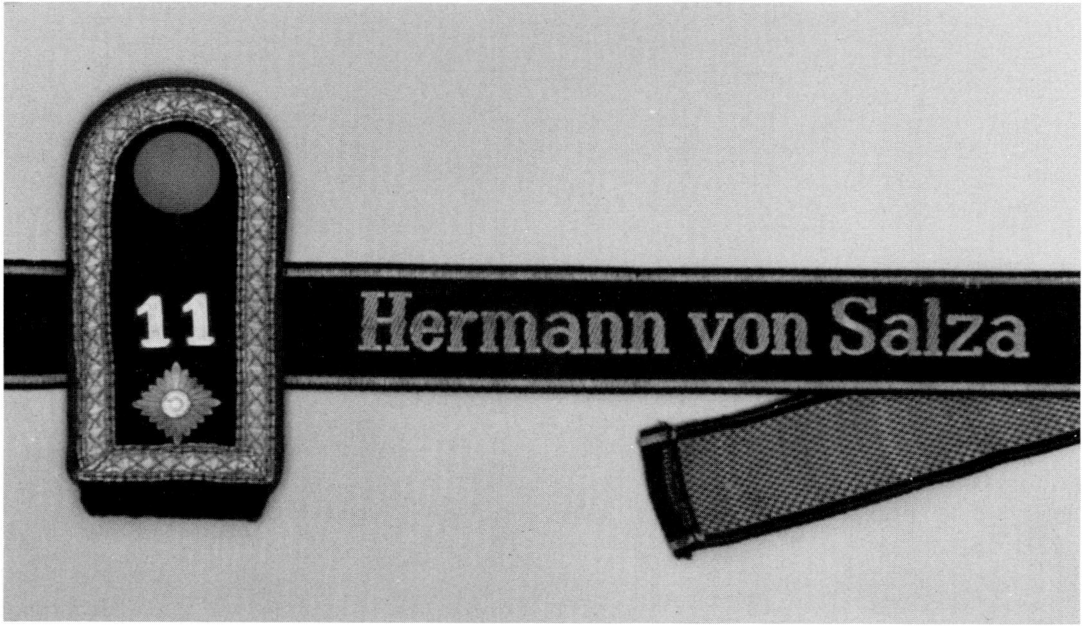

All ranks wore the machine-woven, artificial silk cuff title „Hermann von Salza," The logo, BEVO WUPPERTAL, is evident on the sewn end of the cuff title. The red-piped Oberscharführer shoulder board has the added, and unofficial, Abteilung number "11."

-100-

ᛋᛋ-*Panzer Regiment 12*
12. ᛋᛋ-*Panzer Division „Hitlerjugend"*

„Hitlerjugend" soldiers wore all patterns of the Waffen-ᛋᛋ uniforms, to include those made of Italian Camouflage and the Naval Foul Weather and field caps.

When the division was being formed, between 1,000 to 1,200 soldiers, NCOs, and officers were transferred to the division from the 1. ᛋᛋ-Panzer Division „Adolf Hitler." An order from August 1943 permitted the transfers to continue the wear their „LᛋᛋAH" cuff title. These men took advantage of the order and also continued to wear their LAH shoulder board monograms.

The division received its own cuff title during a ceremony on September 18 and 19, 1944 from Reichsjugendführer (Reich's Youth Leader) Artur Axmann. The issue cuff title was a late-war, machine-woven type with the name „Hitlerjugend" in Latin lettering. A machine-embroidered version in Gothic lettering was seen by former members of the division, but it was an exception and not the rule.

Lernen durch Erfahrung

Issue „Hitlerjugend" cuff titles lack the "salt and pepper" effect on the rear side.

The late-war pattern, machine-woven „Hitlerjugend" cuff title.

SS-Sturmmann Rudi Behme wears the machine-woven „Hitlerjugend" cuff title.

Chapter Four
Waffen-⚡⚡ Panzer Uniform Insignia

⚡⚡-Hauptsturmführer Gentsch, who served with „Prinz Eugen," „Nebelungen," and „L⚡⚡AH," displays Waffen-⚡⚡ shoulder, collar, and sleeve insignia on his service tunic.

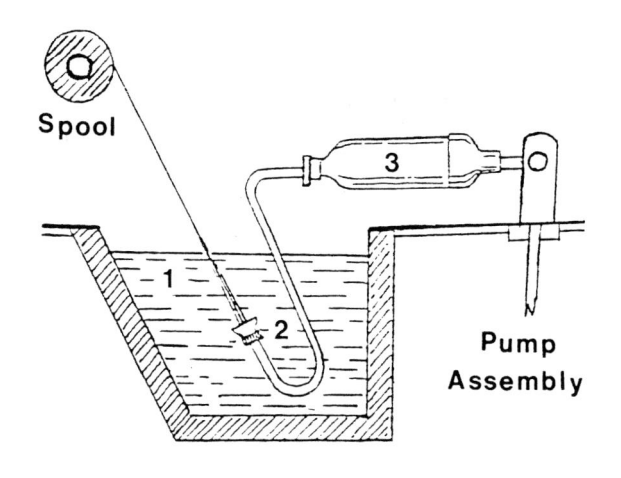

Lernen durch Erfahrung

Artificial Silk

During the war Germany had no access to cotton and did not possess the then highly secret process of producing nylon. Before the war Germany strove for economic independence in many areas, and one aspect of this economic research was the replacement of cotton with rayon, or artificial silk.

The main staple in production of Waffen-// cloth insignia, besides wool, was artificial silk. Artificial silk is produced by pumping a heated and chemically treated cellulose acetate through a nozzle perforated with up to 800 fine holes. The cellulose acetate is obtained from the wood pulp of beechwood and coniferous trees. After the stands shoot out of the nozzle, they are pulled through a chemical bath of sulfuric acid. The thread dries and hardens in pre-warmed air before being rolled onto a spool. The process can produce 100 meters of thread per minute.

Because artificial silk is a natural product, not composed purely of chemicals, it burns like cotton when exposed to a flame. This property makes it ideal for military clothing as synthetics such as nylon melt and stick, which can cause severe burns.

The Waffen-⚡⚡ Cuff Title

The cuff titles worn by individual ⚡⚡-units reflected either their composition, a traditional name, or the name of a historically significant person from German history. The deliberate intent behind the bestowing ⚡⚡ unit with officially named titles is illustrated by the following speech made during the naming ceremony of the 9. ⚡⚡-Panzer Division „Hohenstaufen":

> *A name is similar to a standard; one is presented with it as an individual, unit, or organization. One receives it as a gift, and those who have presented it have expectations, hopes, and objectives. That is why a German title is more than just personal property which one can arbitrarily change or cast aside. It is a commitment of high responsibility.*
>
> *Spirit and life is first given to the name by the wearer. Everyone who wears a named title has the responsibility to assure that the spirit and life of the name is maintained.*
>
> *In German lands there have been men and generations whose names eternally sound out to the German people. These names have become immortal through their great deeds. One such name had been given to our division!*

The Waffen-⚡⚡ wore their cuff titles on the left sleeve of the service uniform, the only uniform intended for their wear, approximately 12cm from the bottom of the cuff. The average cuff title was 49cm long at the time of issue and was 2.5-3cm in width.

The first patterns of cuff titles were machine embroidered for enlisted personnel and hand embroidered for officers and had a 2mm border, each consisting of six to seven aluminum threads on both edges. The name of the unit was machine embroidered in silver gray artificial silk thread or, in the case of officers, hand embroidered in metallic yarn. The size and thickness of the embroidery in cuff titles varies due to the adjustment of the machine or the skill of the individual doing the embroidery.

In 1939 a newer, less expensive cuff title variation was introduced for officers. This cuff title used aluminum thread, machine embroidered into the enlisted style black band. These cuff titles often had a black, artificial silk backing that covered and protected the thread.

The first pattern cuff titles had Gothic style lettering. An order issued in May 1940 changed the lettering style to Latin; the only exception was the LSSAH cuff title, which retained its Sutterlin script „Adolf Hitler." Privately purchased cuff titles in Gothic lettering appeared until the war's end.

The year 1943 saw the introduction of the machine-woven cuff title for enlisted ranks. The entire band was woven in black artificial silk with the Latin letters executed in silver gray. Divisions formed later in the war, such as **Hohenstaufen, Frundsberg,** and **Hitlerjugend**, were issued only this pattern of cuff title. By war's end, all ranks wore this pattern of cuff title.

Examples of the various reverse side and tags found on cuff titles. From the top: first row: Enlisted machine embroidered, with two variations of paper RZM tags in Gothic and Latin lettering. Second row: the 1939 machine woven with aluminum thread and, right, machine-embroidered; both have artificial silk RZM tags. Third row: Machine woven with aluminum thread for officer's and, right, machine woven with artificial silk thread borders for enlisted. Fourth row: the 1943 pattern as produced by BEVO WUPPERTAL and, left, late war, machine-woven pattern.

Two styles of backing found on machine-woven cuff titles. The top example is an officer's pattern with aluminum threads and black artificial silk covering. The "Frundsberg" title is of the machine- woven variety introduced in 1943.

Construction of Waffen-ϟϟ Shoulder Boards

Each Waffen-ϟϟ shoulder board is unique because it is a handmade piece of insignia requiring several sequenced steps of construction. Furthermore, the individuality of the shoulder board is dependent on the rank, material on hand for construction, and the skill of the craftsman. There are two styles of shoulder boards: slip-on and sew-in. The slip-on style has an integral tongue which is slipped through a retaining loop on the shoulder seam of the uniform and secured by a button. The sew-in style is literally sewn into the uniform's shoulder seam.

Black wool was used for the construction of both the top and bottom panels of the main body of the enlisted grade shoulder board. Later in the war, field gray wool was used on the bottom panel of the board. The two panels were sewn together with the branch color piping attached at the edge. A button hole was machine sewn into the board and the tongue of the slip-on style board.

Officer grade shoulder boards were constructed differently. The black wool base was usually sewn around a metal stiffener. The branch color was sandwiched between this base and eight rows of matte aluminum cord on the top. The cord pattern varied between field grade and company grade officers. ϟϟ-officers often wore the more easily obtainable Army pattern shoulder boards, which lacked the black wool underlay beneath in the branch color.

Rank was shown by applying the appropriate tresse and pips. The NCO tresse was available in several variations, from shiny aluminum to dull-gray artificial silk. Normally, Army diamond pattern tresse was used, but when unavailable, Luftwaffe pattern was substituted.

Pips, or stars, exist in numerous variations of high and low detail relief. NCOs wore silver-colored or aluminum pips while officers made use of gilt or bronzed ones. The pips were mounted to the shoulder board with two metal prongs located on the rear. The size of the pip worn on the shoulder board depended on the rank of the individual and whether or not a monogram or unofficial regimental numbers were displayed. The normal size of the pips ranged from 12-15mm.

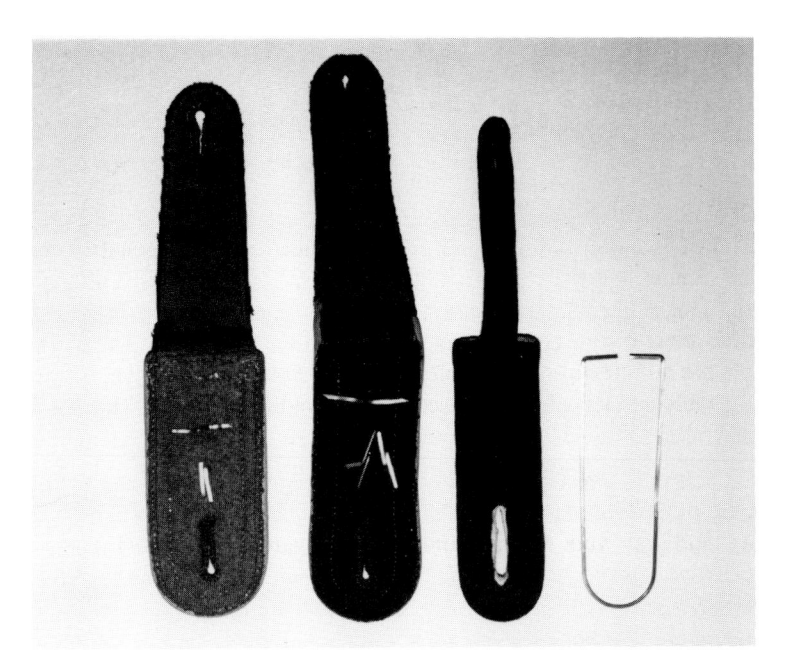

The wire stiffener found inside the Waffen-⚡⚡ officer's shoulder board and the underside of an officer's slip on style shoulder board. Two different enlisted shoulder boards showing different styles of tongues. The metal mounting prongs secure the pips, monograms, or regimental numbers.

Top and bottom views of assorted pips and numbers found on Waffen-⚡⚡ collar and shoulder board insignia.

The Waffen-⚡ Collar Rank Insignia

The Waffen-⚡ displayed the rank on their left side of the uniform collar in addition to that displayed on the shoulder board. The rank collar insignia was a 60 x 40mm parallelogram of black wool moleskin or velvet that used combinations of pips and stripes (see Understanding Waffen-⚡ Ranks and Rank Insignia). Pips used on collar rank insignia were 12mm wide and secured by two metal prongs. Soldiers in the rank of ⚡-Unterscharführer often used a 15mm pip as the sole distinguishing mark on their insignia. The stripes were of 6mm woven aluminum thread with a thin black stripe of black, artificial silk thread running through its middle.

Collar rank insignia was made by folding the cloth face around a stiff buckram or cardboard backing. The backing was saturated with glue produced from animal bones, otherwise known as "bone glue." Sometimes the folded-over cloth ends would also be sewn to increase the durability. Officer's collar rank insignia was fitted with a 1.5mm aluminum twist cord border.

Individual soldiers and officers often added branch piping to their collar insignia, even though Reichsführer-⚡ Himmler had issued an order on November 5, 1940 clearly stating that branch color would be displayed on the shoulder board and field cap only.

The top row shows typical examples of officer pattern collar insignia. Enlisted insignia is shown below. Two types of backing are shown on the left.

An enlarged view of an enlisted rank insignia.

The Waffen-⚡⚡ Collar Runic Insignia

The collar runic insignia was manufactured in the same manner as the rank insignia, with the deletion of rank and the addition of runes. The runes were produced in four different ways:

* Machine woven with artificial silk for enlisted personnel.
* Machine woven with aluminum flatwire for NCOs and, with the addition of 1.5mm aluminum twist cord sewn around the insignia, officers.
* Machine embroidered for enlisted personnel.
* Hand embroidered for NCOs and, with the addition of 1.5mm aluminum twist cord sewn around the insignia, officers.

As with the collar rank insignia, branch piping was often added. While at the front, officers often wore enlisted insignia. The only regiments of ⚡⚡-Panzer Divisions that did not generally wear the collar runic insignia were those of the 3.⚡⚡ PZ Div. „Totenkopf." These units usually wore the distinctive skull on the right side of the collar. Production methods for the Totenkopf were identical to the above.

Officer's hand-embroidered collar runic insignia.

Enlisted machine-embroidered collar runic insignia.

Officer's pattern, machine-woven with aluminum flatwire. This pattern often had a slightly thinner aluminum twist cord sewn around the edge. Below, the enlisted, machine-woven insignia.

An enlarged view of the enlisted, machine-woven runic insignia. This pattern often was backed with cardboard.

An officer's insignia produced by adding aluminum twist cord to an enlisted, machine-woven collar runic insignia (Heinz.)

The Waffen-⚡⚡ Sleeve Eagle

The eagle was the national symbol of the Third Reich and appeared in many forms on the uniforms of its political and military organizations. The predominant difference in the eagle used on the uniforms of the Waffen-⚡⚡ was the way in which the tips came to a point in the middle of the outstretched wing tips. All ⚡⚡ eagles worn on service uniforms had a black background and were sewn centered on the upper left sleeve. Waffen-⚡⚡ Sleeve Eagles were manufactured in the following patterns, of which slight variations of the feather detail existed:

* Officer's hand embroidered. These existed in many variations of detail, depending on the person doing the hand work. This sleeve eagle was generally reserved for the dress uniform, for such fine hand embroidery was easily damaged by wear and tear at the front.
* Enlisted machine embroidered in silver gray artificial silk.
* Officer's machine woven in aluminum thread.
* Enlisted machine woven in silver gray artificial silk. This pattern was also produced using dark green and brown for use on the camouflaged field cap.

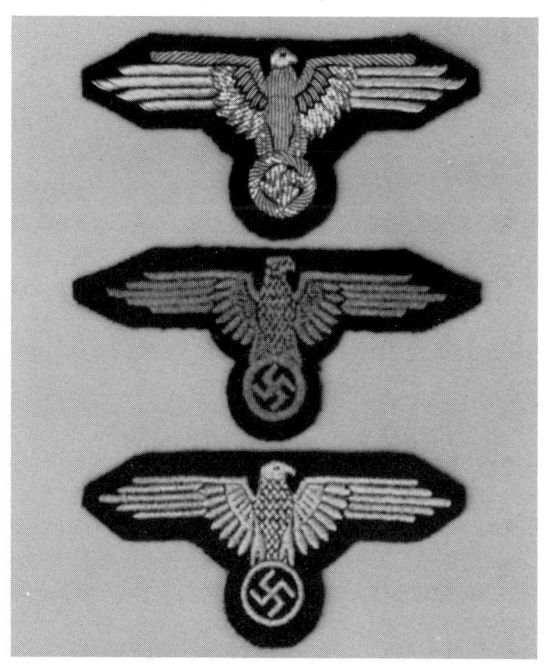

Three examples of embroidered sleeve eagles. The top is an officer's hand-embroidered version. The middle is an early war enlisted pattern and the bottom an enlisted late war pattern.

Detail of an early war, machine-embroidered, enlisted pattern sleeve eagle.

Detail of a late war, machine-embroidered, enlisted pattern sleeve eagle.

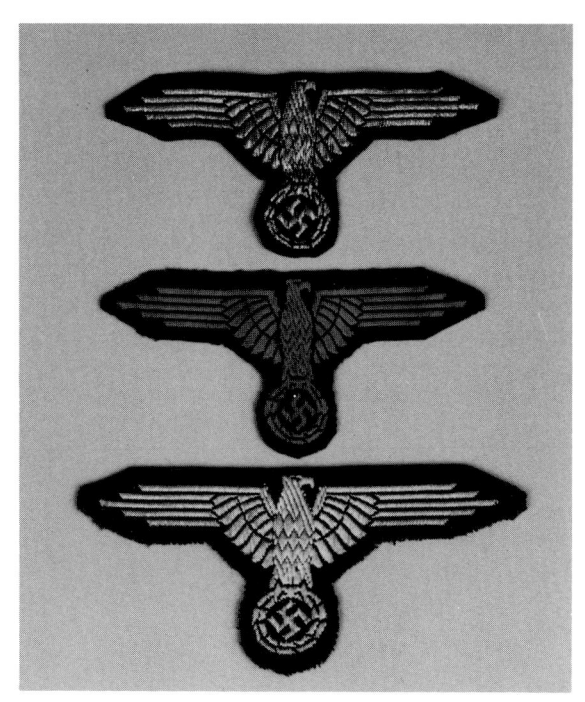

Three machine-woven sleeve eagles. The top is an officer's flat wire pattern. The middle and bottom are enlisted patterns.

Details of a machine-woven Waffen-SS Sleeve Eagle.

-119-

This Waffen-SS Eagle was originally intended for use on the black wool beret worn by early SS Reconnaissance units. This eagle appears from time to time on uniform sleeves and peaked caps. The beret was taken out of service and replaced with the field cap.

The Waffen-ϟϟ Sleeve Rank

Enlisted Waffen-ϟϟ soldiers who were not NCOs wore the following sleeve insignia sewn centered, 1.5cm below the sleeve eagle.

There was no rank insignia for the camouflage uniforms developed for lower enlisted personnel, so these rank insignia were authorized for wear on camouflage uniforms in February 1943.

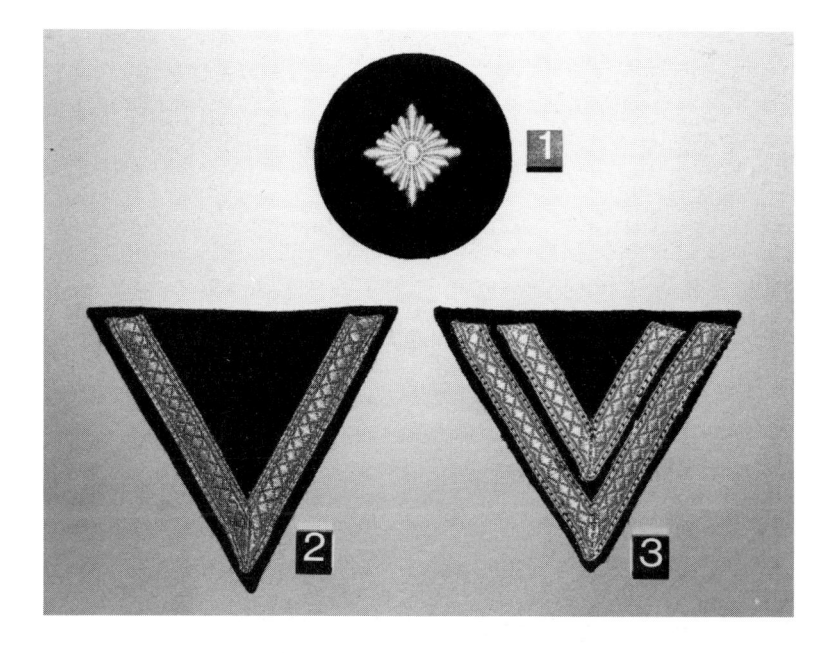

1. ϟϟ-Mann / ϟϟ-Oberschütze, a machine-embroidered, silver-gray star measuring 2cm square on a black, circular background.
2. ϟϟ-Sturmmann, one 9mm tress chevron on triangular black background.
3. ϟϟ-Rottenführer, two 9mm tress chevrons on triangular black background.

The Waffen-SS Rank Insignia for Camouflage Uniforms

In February 1943, a specially designed rank insignia was introduced for NCOs and officers for use on camouflage uniforms. The insignia was intended to solve the problem of rank identification in combat when shoulder boards and collar rank were obscured or camouflage uniforms were in use. The insignia was worn centered 10cm down from the left shoulder seam, but, contrary to regulations, some wore it on both sleeves.

The insignia was manufactured in two methods. The insignia first appeared in a machine embroidered / sewn pattern. The oak leaves were embroidered and the bars cut from a woven tape, then sewn in place. The later pattern were screen printed with black negative on green artificial silk or artificial cotton.

Examples of both patterns of Waffen-SS Rank Insignia for Camouflage Uniforms. Both are for the rank of SS-Sturmbannführer. The top example is machine-embroidered in green artificial silk thread on black wool, and the bottom printed black on green cloth. The cloth used for the base ranged from dark to light shades of green.

The Waffen-⚡⚡ Honor Chevron
(Ehrenwinkel der ⚡⚡)
also known as
The Old Fighters / Campaigners Chevron
(Altekämpfer Winkel)

Although more of an award than a piece of insignia, it is significant because any Waffen-⚡⚡ personnel who had held membership in the ⚡⚡, NSDAP, or other National Socialist organization before January 30, 1933 were entitled to wear it. The chevron was worn centered, 16cm down from the seam on the right sleeve. Austrian volunteers were also authorized to wear the chevron if they had joined the Austrian ⚡⚡ before February 12, 1935.

The chevron was often issued with a small RZM tag which was folded under when sewn to the uniform. Chevrons with the typical paper RZM tag are common in the unissued form. The tag was folded over and around one arm of the chevron and then glued on one end.

Der Alte Hase
On Point With a King Tiger

by Untersturmführer Fritz Kauerauf

At daybreak on the 8th of February 1945, I was ordered to personally report to Obersturmbannführer Paul-Albert Kausch commander of ⚡⚡-Panzer Abteilung 11 „Hermann von Salza." At the time I was 22 years old and an Untersturmführer in the 503 ⚡⚡-Schwere Panzer Abteilung (Heavy tank section) which was attached to the IIIrd Germanic Panzer Corps.

Kausch ordered, "Take a King Tiger and three Sturmgeschütz („Stug") assault guns under the command of Oberscharführer Wild and proceed across the Ihna bridge to Ziegenhagen and Klein-Silber to cut off the reported Russian breakthrough." We then stepped outside of the headquarters and he introduced me to Oshar. Wild and wished us luck on our mission.

I took command of Usha. Lindl's King Tiger. I already knew his crew very well. Lindl drove with us for a while but eventually he stayed behind.

From the command post, which was south of Jakobshagen to behind the hills west of the Ihna, we drove on. After driving up the hills we saw before us quite a spectacle. An endless Russian column, from south to north, on the heights east of the Ihna, with tanks, artillery, vehicles of every type, and even horse drawn units.

Oshar. Wild was a specialist in successful tank attacks. He had been presented with the Knights Cross in Kurland in 1944 by Field Marshal Model. Wild agreed with me that something had to be done immediately "because if they advance further to the Baltic Sea, the troops in Kurland would be cut off before they complete their withdrawal by sea to Stettin." With only our four tanks we were too weak of a force to go up against the overwhelming enemy forces, so I sent Wild back to get reinforcements.

In a short time he returned with two King Tigers under the command of Obersturmführer Kaes, and ten more Sturmgeschütz (Stug) assault guns from the 1st ⚡⚡-Panzer Abteilung „Hermann von Salza." A company of paratroopers accompanied them. With these reinforcements we also had a few more Stugs from the Nordland Division's 11th Sturmgeschütz Abteilung, commanded by Sturmbannführer Schulz-Streek. We departed around noon in the direction of Ziegenhagen. Before we reached the Ihna River, we had to knock out an antitank gun situated on the outskirts of

Ziegehagen. Straddling both sides of the small Ihna bridge the paratroopers crossed over, with us following behind. There were two Stugs in front of us.

The town was penetrated and house to house fighting started. We turned left on the street, then went into a right curve where both Stugs were halted in a firefight with a Russian antitank gun that was positioned near the church. The antitank gun was at a range of 150-200 meters, blocking us from the main street which led to the columns of advancing Russian convoys. Neither the Stugs nor the antitank gun could hit one another because of a small rise in the middle of the street. At this point the battle became a stalemate.

Untersturmführer Fritz Kauerauf

With the greater height of our King Tiger, it was up to us to get the attack back in gear. One of the Stug commanders told me the exact position of the antitank gun. Seconds after the antitank gun fired a round, we swung our tank around the corner and put the surprised antitank crew out of action.

We advanced immediately, with Ostrm. Kaes' two King Tigers and Wild's assault guns following behind. Now the success of the attack depended on us. Soon, though, we were stopped once more. This time a minefield was spread out between two houses that were parallel to one another. Russian small arms picked up on our tank. The Russians noticed us by the empty shell casings we chucked out from the tank. The paratroopers fought beside of us from a house, protecting us at the same time. However the village was still in the hands of the Russians.

My request for Pioniers to remove the minefield did not meet with success. I thought I would have to climb out and do it myself, which was easier said then done. Help came from an unidentified officer who had a clothing bag full of explosives. He was in dress uniform! Possibly he was just out of the hospital? Anyway, he ran beside of our tank and took cover behind the house on the right side that had the mines lying in the open. He began detonating the mines with hand grenades and explosives. He did this 5-10 times and we gave him cover as best as we could with our on-board machine guns. The unknown Untersturmführer put on quite a performance.

He then assisted us in another decisive way. Noticing a hidden threat down a street that was blind to us, he gesticulated wildly to get my attention. He pointed up the street. I had the loader pull out the 120cm long high explosive round and replace it with an armor piercing round. Thank God, because a muzzlebrake that could only belong to a Josef Stalin tank poked out from the backside of a house. The monster then rolled right in front of us at a range of 50 meters. *"12 O'clock, armor piercing, Josef Stalin, between hull and turret, Aim, fire!"* I ordered. Fritz Lukesch fired. The Russian tank stopped immediately and the hatches flew open. My crew cheered. But the enemy tank's gun barrel was still pointed at us, so I yelled through the tank *"Gone crazy!! Put in another round—then another."* The Stalin was now burning in bright flames, with its ammunition exploding. Next we saw two more Stalin tanks approaching to the left of the one we just shot. Their crews were so shocked, that they climbed out of their vehicles and ran away. We didn't fire on these two tanks because their gun barrels were still pointing upwards. It was obvious that they hadn't counted on us being there and had never seen a King Tiger up close. The paratroopers waved happily at us and congratulated us over the radio.

Then it was time to move on again. After the flames of the burning monster had subsided, we squeezed on past and found ourselves on the main road of the Russian advance. The Russians scattered in fright and the road was ours. Oscha. Wild and the other tanks were still with us.

We fought our way forward—escorted by the paratroopers—already knowing that our mission was a success. By this time, we had already been hit two or three times by enemy rounds, all of which bounced off. In any case, the Russian advance to the north was crushed.

That evening we were at the southern exit of Klein-Silber, which led to Reetz. There we secured ourselves for the night with the other two King Tigers. There were only about seven paratroopers with us, barely enough to put out two machine gun posts. The paratroopers had performed well that day and were really worn out, but they held out.

Kaes and I attempted to find the forward command post on foot that night. It proved impossible because all hell broke loose in the village behind us. We were all saddened to find out that the unknown Ustuf. who had destroyed the minefield and warned us about the enemy tanks had been killed by a mortar round. We had thought he would have received the Knights Cross for his brave actions.

Later that night we found a supply truck and each King Tiger got a 200-liter barrel of gasoline. There was no food—but no one was hungry anyway. Refueling the tanks with the barrels of fuel was bone-breaking work. In the meantime, a few stray Russians and a riderless horse and wagon ran through the area.

To rest up a bit we spread ourselves out inside of the compact interior of the tank. One of us kept a constant watch in the commander's cupola. We hardly slept because the artillery of the Russians, who had been pushed back, kept shelling the village. Shortly before morning came we got the order to take the rest of the village on the eastern side. We had to maneuver the tank back about 100 meters. Contrary to previous plans, there was a misunderstanding and we ended up once again as the point tank.

The situation didn't look good for a successful armored assault. To us it just didn't seem necessary. The area could be occupied through other means. That's what happened later. This time we wouldn't have needed infantry support from the paratroopers that we enjoyed the day before. Over the radio I repeatedly requested "Sand rabbits" (code name for infantry), but it was no use. All I received were more orders to attack. I called down to the driver. "Menke, do we drive or not?!" The whole crew answered back in chorus, "Untersturmführer we are going!" I found out later that our whole conversation was heard over the net and General Steiner's Staff section heard it, besides the Russians frequencies they were monitoring. They commended us but my crew would never find out.

I said over the radio, "Eagle one to Rainbow, sitting on the village exit, please follow!" and to my driver "Menke move us out at top speed to the village exit." It was only about 500-600 meters away. I had hoped the other tanks and assault guns would follow behind us. It turned out we found ourselves completely alone on the outskirts of the village. I tried to make contact by radio but to no avail. My orders weren't being followed. I asked over the radio if we were supposed to turn back, but an answer never came back. We could not understand why we weren't being answered. Later, as I was in the military hospital, I found out that Ostuf. Kaes' King Tiger had been set on fire by the Russians, therefore blocking the street so that the assault guns could no longer follow. Kaes and his crew were lucky and survived the ordeal.

We were now sitting at the outskirts of the village alone. After 15 minutes we could no longer wait, for no one had followed us. We slowly turned back, firing from time to time with our machine guns. Half-way back, we were confronted with a road block made of wagons and farm equipment. The Russians had set it up during the time we had waited for the other tanks. We tried to slowly drive around it, but the left rear side of the tank slipped, causing the main gun to point skywards. Our machine guns were rendered useless. Using ladders the Russians immediately started trying to climb onto the tank. We were momentarily helpless.

I ordered the driver to give full gas and to get back on the main street so we could go through a passage between some farm buildings and get out of the village. It appeared as if we would succeed. We were almost out when a forceful detonation shook the tank. There was flash fire and the tank immediately stood still. *"Get out and away!"* I yelled down through the tank. As I was climbing out, a second round penetrated the turret and smashed my lower left leg. A third hit followed. As I sprang from the tank, I saw one of my crewman running away from the wrecked vehicle; in reality two other crewman escaped. They made their way back to the position we had occupied the night before. A Sturmgeschütz and one of the King Tigers were still there. The King Tiger was immobilized due to a failure in its electric system. It could only use its two on-board machine guns.

Our paratroopers from the day before were also there. I found all this out, later. In full view of the Russians, I collapsed in front of our destroyed tank. As I laid there I pulled my pistol out of my trouser pocket. The Russians weren't concerned with me; the sight of the burning King Tiger was more important. Inside were our Kameraden: Fritz Lukesch the gunner, 17, from the seven mountains region in Romania. The loader, Bruno Tuschkewitz, believed to the last that his Pommeranian homeland could be reconquered. Now they were both dead; the King Tiger was their grave.

I saw the radioman escape, and the driver got away with a few burns. The front of our tank could be seen from the Stug that both of my crewmen had escaped to, and they soon realized that I was lying there. I started crawling to a small animal stall situated between two houses which was separated by a wood plank door. Our Sturmgeschütz and the Russians sprang to action. The Stug began firing its gun into the surrounding farm buildings. They always fired further ahead so I wouldn't get hit by shrapnel or splinters. The Russians were forced to take cover. I had time to bind my wounded leg using the cable from my headphones and a piece of wood. I was not in great pain, but my foot was severely twisted in the wrong direction. I was still wearing the shoe, but my leather trousers were shredded. Lying on my stomach, I waved to the Sturmgeschütz. Suddenly there was a stabbing pain in my upper legs. Behind me a Russian stood firing a submachine gun from the hip. His first two shots had hit me, but because of the weapons recoil he lost his aim as the burst tore to the left. I shot him down with my pistol. Another Russian who was glancing around the corner met the same fate. He was dragged away by his feet. I laid on my back and watched both corners of the stall. No Russian showed himself, but a grenade was thrown around the corner and landed on my lower body. I grabbed it and cast it away. Just as it left my hand it exploded. My lower lip was struck by a 4-5cm metal strip. It was stuck under my lower front teeth. I pulled it out and gave a loud cry so the Russians would finally think I was dead. Another Russian appeared from around the corner, but I promptly shot him down. Three men from the Stug were approaching me. They were looking around as if they were searching for me. The Russians behind the houses I was hiding between had apparently also seen them. I remained silent, hoping that the Russians would think I was dead. The men from the Stug were nearly within calling range but turned back. I felt very depressed and crawled over to the plank wood door. On the other side stood two Russians and a Russian heavy machine gun with an ammunition drum mounted on the top of it. They could not hear me because the loud din of the surrounding fighting was to loud. My second magazine was already loaded in the pistol, so I aimed it through a crack in the door and opened up on the two Russians—keeping in mind that I must save one bullet for myself.

As fate would have it, things turned out completely different than what I had expected. I aimed-fired, aimed-fired, and aimed again but the action locked back—*empty!* I cast away the pistol and started crawling as fast as I could. I commanded all of my strength and kept on crawling past where the Sturmgeschütz was. I hid beneath a bunch of potato leaves and passed out.

When I came to my senses I could see a cloudy sky and a Russian „Rata" (fighter plane). At the end of my street stood a paratrooper, firing an assault rifle up into the air. Two of my men in leather uniforms called to me, *"Untersturmführer, where can we pick you up?"* I cried back *"by the shoulders, let's get out of here!"* Without stopping, they carried me about 200-300 meters through the field to a Sturmgeschütz. Only after we were safely aboard the Sturmgeschütz did the covering paratrooper join us. The commander of our third King Tiger came to the Sturmgeschütz and informed me that his tank was no longer usable. On my order he blew up the breech and lit the tank on fire.

At 9:30 the next morning I was dropped off at the main dressing station. After the war I could only find out about one of the men who had rescued me. He died in the battle for Berlin. Someone had found his Soldbuch[1] (pay book) and I sent it to his parents with no return address. In his last letter he wrote that his tank had to be destroyed and all of his things were burned up. *"God bless you"* were his last words to his parents.

As I was being loaded into the medical truck that would take me from the main dressing station to the hospital, two men from Sturmgeschütz Section 11 who were standing nearby exclaimed, *"Untersturmführer we saw everything. Get well soon!"* In the Hospital I heard that the Grenadiers of the Nordland Division were occupying the area we had taken; therefore, it was possible to withdraw from surrounded Arnswalde about a week later. Some of the surviving King Tigers from ₦-Panzer Abteilung 503 were brought by train to defend Danzig!

Knights Cross holder Oscha. Phillip Wild came to the hospital after being heavily wounded when his tank was shot up during the breakthrough to Arnswalde. The dramatic attack that Kausch, Wild, and I undertook did not go unobserved. After the war in late 1945, while in the district hospital Ratzeburg, Below Kaserne, (British guarded ₦-hospital), I was informed by a Hauptsturmführer from the staff of ₦-AOK 11 (Steiner)[2] that while monitoring the Russian radio frequency, they became overjoyed as they heard the mass panic we had inflicted on the Russians and the victory of the King Tiger at the point when it defeated the three Josef Stalin tanks during the successful attack on the Russian's main advance route.

Footnotes

[1] Soldbuch i.e.; Pay book. Every German Serviceman was issued a small booklet which contained all the pertinent information on the individual such as, family, rank and promotions, blood type, medical information, awards, weapons and clothing issue, leaves, and payment.

[2] The Nordland Division and the III Germanic Panzerkorps fell under the command of ₦-Obergruppenführer and General of the Waffen-₦, Felix Steiner.

Der Alte Hase

ᛋᛋ-Panzers in Normandy; An ᛋᛋ-Panzer Platoon Leader in the Roncey Pocket, July 1944.

by Major Stephen M. Rusiecki

On 20 July 1944, the U.S. First Army successfully broke out from Normandy's hedgerows at St. Lô. The Americans quickly raced south and then east, creating chaos among the ranks of the startled German units. Many of these German units began withdrawing east toward the Seine River. Among them was the 2nd ᛋᛋ Panzer Division „Das Reich," which had marched north from southern France in response to the Normandy invasion. The division was fighting just east of Coutances, a French city southwest of St. Lô. Threatened with imminent encirclement, the remnants of „Das Reich" moved east as well, away from the American tanks that were exploiting their newly won maneuver space.

ᛋᛋ-Untersturmführer Fritz Langanke, a Mark V Panther platoon leader in ᛋᛋ-Panzer Regiment "Das Reich," found himself embroiled in the chaos created by the American breakout at St. Lô. By 29 July, the entire 2nd ᛋᛋ Panzer Division „Das Reich" was regrouping for a deliberate breakout from the American encirclement already rapidly taking shape. The 29th of July became one of Fritz Langanke's longest days in combat, but it was also his most successful. By the time the sun would rise on 30 July, Langanke would earn the coveted Knight's Cross of the Iron Cross for his part in leading the breakout.

Langanke's day began at midnight on 29 July. His company commander had led his platoon away from the fighting to Savigny, a small hamlet southeast of Coutances. In Savigny, elements of the 2nd ᛋᛋ-Panzer Division were regrouping before moving east and out of the rapidly forming pocket. As part of a new task organization, Langanke's platoon was attached to the 3rd Battalion, ᛋᛋ-Panzer-Grenadier Regiment „Deutschland." The battalion's mission included gathering as many Wehrmacht units as possible and leading them from the pocket. Cloaked in the safety of the night's precious darkness, Langanke's Panther tank led the battalion south, followed by other elements of "Das Reich." The battalion commander, ᛋᛋ-Sturmbannführer Helmut Schreiber, rode on Langanke's Panther.

Untersturmführer Fritz Langanke

The column raced southeast, the night protecting them from Allied air attacks. The direction of movement focused on the small French town of Percy, just south of the east-west Route Nationale D-13, an improved dirt road the division would have to cross. As Langanke's Panther approached D-13 at la Croix-Marie, a startling sight met his eyes. German staff cars and dozens of other vehicles clogged the east-west artery, creating an impossible traffic jam. Schreiber leapt from Langanke's tank, reconnoitered forward, and discovered an American roadblock on the highway.

Schreiber directed Langanke to eliminate the roadblock; the Americans manning it had no armor with them. Langanke, eager to comply, dismounted from his tank. Empty buses, staff cars, and radio vehicles blocked his path. The drivers ignored Langanke's pleas to return to their cars and move them. No other combat units were in the area. Disgusted, Langanke grabbed some radios from a staff car, placed them behind his turret for later use, and drove over the vehicles blocking his path. The American resistance quickly crumbled; the GIs had only one anti-tank gun to threaten Langanke. This weapon was no match for Langanke's Panther.

Langanke informed Schreiber of his success; the road was now clear. But, to Langanke's dismay, Schreiber and other officers were busy turning the division's vehicles west. They wanted to cross D-13 farther west, near the town of Lengronne. Langanke pleaded for them to abandon this senseless plan, but to no avail. By now, the sun was out and American „Jabos" (fighter planes) would soon darken the sky overhead. Langanke organized his platoon and moved west, again leading the division's main column. Langanke drove for two hours, unmolested by Allied aircraft. The planes were attacking targets of opportunity in the distance. „Das Reich" would almost certainly be next.

Langanke's Panther soon approached a crossroads southeast of Roncey called la Valtolaine. Suddenly, American Sherman tanks, moving north from Hambye toward Roncey, blocked Langanke's path. Within minutes, dozens of „Jabos" blackened the sky. Bombs exploded everywhere, shattering the division's staff cars and other equipment. The Allied planes unleasned their full fury upon the lone intersection. A few staff cars moved off the road and into the hedgerows. Langanke buttoned up inside his Panther. His three other Panther crews followed suit.

The Allied air attack was devastating. Langanke's Panthers could do nothing but sit in the open and hope against a direct hit. Thankfully, the bombers weren't particularly accurate on point targets. Fear and anxiety gripped Langanke and his crew. The hot, stifling environment in the tank compounded the crew's stress. Langanke and his men were near their breaking points. Suddenly, shrapnel ignited the radios Langanke had liberated from the radio car several hours earlier. They burned brightly. Langanke popped his hatch and pushed them to the ground, burning his hand. An American pilot saw this action and dove straight for Langanke's Panther. Other planes joined in. The bombing concentration that followed was so severe that Langanke and his crew inside the tank saw dents appear in the tank's armor from the force of the explosions outside.

Suddenly, there was a sharp bang. Daylight appeared inside the Panther. Wiping dust from his eyes, Langanke realized that the shock of the bombs had blown free a metal plate in the turret that covered a mounting hole for a small, turret-mounted mortar. The mortars, designed to ward off dismounted infantry, were unavailable, so a metal plate covered the hole. The shock of the „Jabos"' bombs had sheered off the retaining bolts. Instinctively, Langanke and his loader stuffed their bedrolls into the hole. More shrapnel blew the blankets back out, but finally they remained in place.

Langanke's gunner soon reached his breaking point. Forced to observe the events outside through his gunsight, the gunner quickly lost his composure. He had witnessed the bombs' effects on a platoon of German paratroopers just outside the tank. The bombs killed the soldiers instantly. However, repeated bombings dismembered and disemboweled the corpses before the gunner's very eyes. A decapitated head rolled onto the crossroads. The gunner shouted and swore in horror. He tried to force himself from the turret, but Langanke rammed his pistol into the man' s neck and screamed, *"Shut your damn mouth, or I'll blow your rotten nut off!"* The gunner quickly regained his composure.

Langanke, close to his breaking point as well, chose to reposition the tank for better cover. He instructed the driver to move the Panther at a right angle and break through the hedgerow. The tank would either get through or break a drive sprocket. The Panther made it and, after moving for 100 meters to some cover, stopped. Langanke and the crew dismounted. The „Jabos" had lost interest and left. The crew, glad to be free of the tank' s hot, claustrophobic interior, rested under the vehicle's hull for an hour.

By early afternoon, the area had become quiet. Langanke set out on foot to find ᛋᛋ-Sturmbannführer Schreiber. He learned that the American tanks they encountered earlier had blocked and cut off Schreiber and the rest of the division. Only some remnants remained with Langanke and his platoon. The survivors looked to Langanke for leadership, and he quickly devised a plan for a nighttime breakout. He gathered all functioning equipment and vehicles and lined them up near the road. His Panthers made gaps in the hedgerows so the column could bypass the destruction that littered and clogged the la Valtolaine intersection. Langanke found a regimental command post belonging to a German Army unit, but the officers, all senior to Langanke, refused to organize or to participate in a breakout. Most of them seemed content with surrendering. Disgusted and ashamed of his own military, Langanke stormed out of the command post.

At 2200 hours on 29 July, Langanke formed up his motley band of ⚡⚡ soldiers, Army soldiers, and paratroopers. The column consisted of Langanke' s Panther in the lead followed by a Panzer Mark IV, two Sturmgeschützen (assault guns), the flak battalion of ⚡⚡-Panzer-Grenadier Regiment „Deutschland" (five 3.7cm self-propelled guns), two 10.5 cm self-propelled artillery pieces, all of „Deutschland's" remaining wheeled vehicles, about thirty trucks, and Langanke' s remaining Panther. The „Jabos" had destroyed his other two.

The column ran a gauntlet of American tank and small arms fire as it moved east and crossed D-58, the north-south road that formed part of the la Valtolaine crossroads. Firing on the move and destroying enemy tanks and other forms of resistance, Langanke's Panther forged ahead in the darkness. Several paratroopers riding on the outside of the tanks and assault guns became casualties, but the column remained intact as it forged east. When the sun rose on the morning of 30 July, Langanke's column was free of the impending American encirclement. He had saved a substantial amount of equipment and men to fight another day. For his leadership and skill in organizing and conducting the breakout, Fritz Langanke received the Knight' s Cross of the Iron Cross. His adventure in the "Pocket of Roncey," as the Germans call it, was over, but he had earned the admiration and respect of his fellow soldiers and officers. Even today, Fritz Langanke's status as a true ⚡⚡ Panzer officer remains unquestionable.

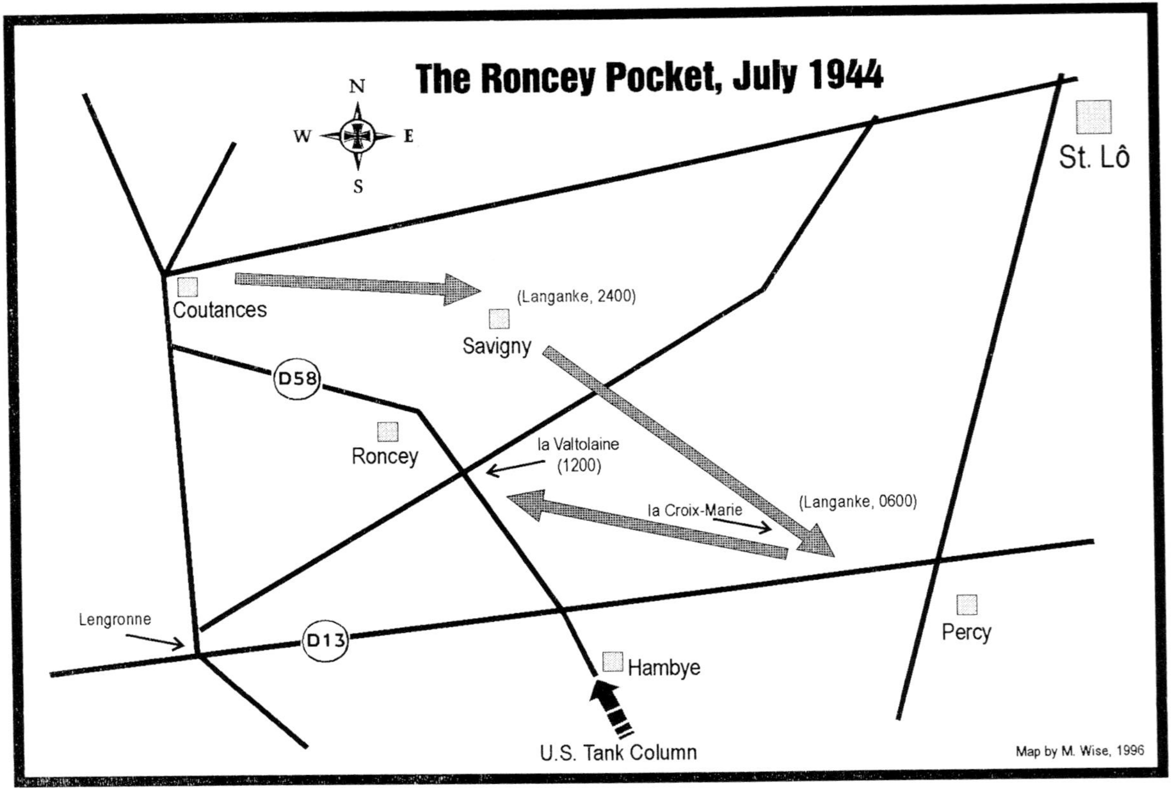

-136-

Author's Biography

A native of Milwaukee, Wisconsin, Richard Mundt is an armor enthusiast, model builder, and collector of Waffen-*ff* Panzer uniforms and related militaria. He lived in Germany for ten years, four of which were spent in the U.S. Army serving his country as a tank crewman on M60A1 and M60A3 tanks.

Mr. Mundt reads and speaks fluent German and has, as a guest, attended numerous gatherings and reunions conducted by former veterans of the Waffen-*ff*. At these gatherings, which ranged from company level to corps level, he has taken the opportunity to interview a number of former Waffen-*ff* tankers first hand.

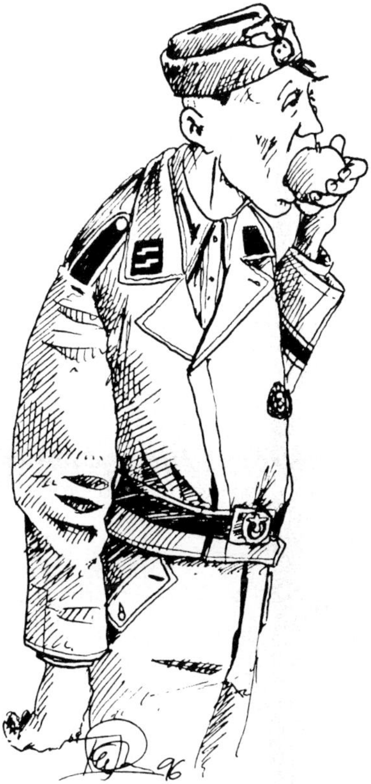